UNSTOPPABLE FAVOR

God's Plan & God's way

Written By:

Dr. Sheka Mansaray

Revelation Publishing
Kingdom Revelation fit to print

Dedication & Acknowledgements

.

I acknowledge the almighty God for His amazing and unstoppable blessing, grace, favor, wisdom, vision, insight and faith in my life. I sincerely acknowledge my beautiful wife Dr. Nanah Mansaray for standing beside me throughout the writing of this book.

To my son, Joseph Ezekiel Mansaray this book is dedicated to you, you are my favor and my Increase I love you so much.

To all "Faith Embassy International Ministries – Revelation Church-" Branches around the world, thank you family for all of your support and prayer, And to my children, daughter, Faith Mansaray; and Son, Sheka Jeremiah Mansaray Jr and son, Joseph Ezekiel Mansaray.

Joseph was thirty years old when he stood before Pharaoh king of Egypt. And Joseph went out from the presence of Pharaoh and went throughout all the land of Egypt. Genesis 41:46

But the LORD was with Joseph, and shewed him mercy, and gave him favour in the sight of the keeper of the prison. Genesis 39:21

And I will grant this people such favor in the sight of the Egyptians that when you leave, you will not go away empty-handed. Exodus 3:21

Table of Contents

Poem: Do Me A Favor

Come do me this favor
It's your turn to received unstoppable favor
To be so compliant;
Is just amazing in itself!
I was favored by God
His Favor turn me out for Good
God's witness so that all can see,
His only son died for me
So they can come to the place,
To accept His Grace.
Come do me this favor
It's your turn to received unstoppable favor
Came an angel with a word called favor
The disgrace of an unwed mother called Mary
The thought of Her fiancé may leave her;
The aftermath of the disgrace called grace
they, came from a far place
to see or received a blessing or even peace
they were once salt now Lost His flavor
they came to see a word called favor
Unstoppable Favor
Come do me this favor
It's your turn to received unstoppable favor
gracious kindness
His flavor is unstoppable sweetness

an advantage to the benefit of someone approve;
consider as the favorite;

promote over another

bestow a privilege upon

treat gently or carefully

Come do me this favor

It's your turn to received unstoppable favor

You can never win with sin

With Jesus you can only win

God reformed my heart,

God had favor me at my worst,

He allows me to recognize new start. He helps me from sins to depart,

His Spirit, now in my heart.

Come do me this favor

It's your turn to received unstoppable favor

The day has come to enter into favor, husband or wife,

Children and parents, both He gave life

And if anyone contracts disease or becomes very ill.

God's favor will rest on that person still. Come do me this favor

It's your turn to received unstoppable favor

Introduction

I know like everyone you have a thought about favor and how can you be a partaker of such level of honor and blessing. Well I believe you have in your hand the first steps to manifest Unstoppable favor.... Unstoppable favor is something that God releases upon His people. This is one of His blessings that He grants us. In this book you will understand the simple study, together we will explore what Unstoppable favor is, what it brings into our lives and what we can do to receive Unstoppable favor.

• What is Unstoppable favor?
• What happens when the favor of God is upon us?
• What causes the favor of God to come upon us? Unstoppable favor is an endowment of God that is released upon a person and gives the person influence, access to people, places or things, unusual opportunities, exaltation and divine intervention.

The Bible talks about God being impartial (Romans 2:11; Acts 10:34).
For there is no partiality with God (Romans 2:11).

All our lives, you and I have sought the FAVOR of someone.

*Remember when we were little kids, how we would color or draw a picture and take it to our mom or dad for their approval? We were seeking their favor.

* Did you ever have a FAVORITE teacher in grade school or High School? Remember how much harder we worked in that

teacher's class? It was because we wanted to FIND FAVOR in their eyes.

* And who among us here today didn't do some pretty stupid stuff when we were teenagers........to try to impress our friends or some boy or girl we really liked? It was because we wanted to FIND FAVOR in their eyes.

(STOP) Think deeply about this and position yourself in it...

Now God had caused the official to show favor and compassion to Daniel, Daniel 1:9

But the LORD was with Joseph, and shewed him mercy, and gave him favour in the sight of the keeper of the prison. Genesis 39:21

"But Noah found favor in the eyes of the Lord." "But Noah found favor in the eyes of the Lord."

NOAH has always been one of my favorite PEOPLE IN THE BIBLE. If you were like me, you probably first heard the story of Noah and the Ark when you were sitting in church on a Sunday morning receiving education by a Sunday School teacher.

Because we learned of NOAH at such an early age, there is a tendency to think of NOAH as a Story Book Character, rather than a real, live human being. BUT we know God's Word is true........and the BIBLE teaches us that NOAH was a real person who once walked on this earth, just like you and me.

Besides the fact he built the Ark, what else do we know about NOAH?

We learn in Genesis 5: 28, 29 that Noah's father's name was LAMECH ......who was 182 years old when NOAH was born. Can you imagine a 182-year-old man down on the floor wrestling with a little toddler?

Going back even farther in NOAH'S FAMILY TREE we discover in Genesis 5:26 that Noah was the grandson of Methusaleh, who still holds the distinction of being the oldest human being who ever lived.

We also learn in Genesis 6:18 that NOAH was married, although the scriptures never mention the name of his wife. We have always affectionately referred to her as "Mrs. Noah."

Genesis 5: 32 tells us that when NOAH was 500 years old, he and the Mrs. had three sons......Shem, Ham and Japheth. And that each of them eventually married.

Of course, we know it was these EIGHT members of Noah's family, God spared aboard the Ark, when he destroyed the world with a catastrophic flood.

But more important than all this BIOGRAPHICAL data about NOAH, was NOAH'S character.

6:8,9 But Noah found favor in the eyes of the Lord. This is the account of Noah. Noah was a righteous man, blameless among the people of his time, and he walked with God.

Now contrast the life of Noah with the way the rest of the world was living at that time. (Genesis 6:5-7)

6:5 The Lord saw how great man's wickedness on the earth had become, and that every inclination of the thoughts of his heart was only evil all the time.

6:6 The Lord was grieved that he had made man on earth, and his heart was filled with pain.
6:7 So the Lord said, "I will wipe mankind, whom I have created, from the face of the earth---men and animals, and creatures that move along the ground, and birds of the air---for I am grieved that I have made them."

Now   listen   again   to   verse   8..........
6:8 But Noah found favor in the eyes of the Lord.

In the TEN GENERATIONS that had passed from the time Adam and Eve committed the very first sin in the Garden of Eden to the days of Noah, man had completely turned his mind and heart away from GOD and toward sin.

VERSE 5 said........." every inclination of the thoughts of his heart was only evil all the time."

The whole world was "BLANKETED IN THE DARKNESS OF SIN" ....but in all this darkness, there stood one man who's life shone like a bright star.........And that man was NOAH.........A RIGHTEOUS MAN ....A BLAMELESS MAN.........A MAN WHO WALKED WITH GOD.

What is Favour

Your servant has indeed found favor in your sight, and you have shown me great Kindness by saving my life. But I can't run to the mountains; the disaster will overtake me, and I will die. Genesis 19:19

"Please say that you are my sister so that it may go well with me because of you, and that I may live on account of you." Genesis 12:13
Bless the LORD, O my soul, And all that is within me, bless His holy name. Psalm 103:1-22

After these things I looked, and behold, a door standing open in heaven, and the first voice which I had heard, like the sound of a trumpet speaking with me, said, "Come up here, and I will show you what must take place after these things." Revelation 4:1

1)   To show favour is to show kindness. It is to give a helping hand.
2)   Favour is unmerited mercy, blessing and kindness.
3)   Favour is open-heavens, open doors and divine connection.
4)   Favour is the reward for a good service done.
5)   Favour is access to heavenly blessings.
6)   Favour is the secret, hidden and unspoken dream of every human living today. We strive for it, and even beg for it.
7)   Favour can turn tragedy into triumph within moments.
8)   Favour births success.

9)   Favour moved Joseph from the prison to the palace of Pharaoh in one day.

10)   Favour is the miracle of God in operation. It always leaves a man excited, happy and full of praises.

11)   Favour is when God causes someone to desire to become a problem-solver in your life. It may be a relative, your boss, or a stranger. According to the scriptures, God is the one behind the linking and connection with someone who blesses you.

12)   Favour is a gift from God that can stop if not recognized and appreciated properly.

13)   Favour is an attitude of goodness toward you, not an exchange or payment for something you have done. God does not owe you. Others are not obligated to you. No man can stop the favour of God from reaching you.

14)   "He opens and no man can close it" (Rev. 3:7).

15)   Exchange is a transaction, which can come through intimidation or obligation.

16)   Favour is a gift that comes from a free-willed heart.

17)   Favour is not an accident, but a deliberate design by God to reward you for acts of obedience invisible to others.

18)   "If ye be willing and obedient, ye shall eat the good of the land" (Isaiah 1:19).

19)   Favour is often the only exit from a place of captivity and bondage.

20)   God uses favour to bring man out of a tight corner into freedom and success.

21)   Joseph knew this, so he requested favour from the butler.

22)   Though delayed for two years, it eventually came when it was God's time to favour him.

23)   Favour is an exception to the rule, not normality. Millions struggle without seeing significant progress. "Except the Lord build the house, they labour in vain that build it".

Recognize Favour

But Joseph had recognized his brothers, although they did not recognize him. Genesis 42:8

He did not recognize him, because his hands were hairy like his brother Esau's hands; so he blessed him. Genesis 27:23

That all the peoples of the earth may know that the hand of the LORD is mighty, so that you may fear the LORD your God forever." Joshua 4:24

(1) Success will require favour from someone. You cannot work hard enough to get everything you deserve. You need favour to be debt free, and to accomplish your dreams.

"The LORD thy God shall bless thee in all thine increase, and in all the works of thine hands". (Deut.16:15).

(2) Favour can make you wealthy in a single day. Ruth experienced this when Boaz married her and all that was Boaz's became hers.

"So Boaz took Ruth, and she was his wife" (Ruth 4:13).

The wealth of Abraham was transferred to Rebecca through Isaac in a single day.

(3) Favour can silence a lifetime enemy forever. Haman was hung after the king showed Mordecai and Queen Esther favour.

(4) Favour can make you a household name in a day. The king made Esther Queen, and a "nobody" became a "somebody" in a single day (Esther 2:16).

(5) Favour can double your financial worth in the midst of your worst tragedy. It happened to Job. "The LORD blessed the latter end of Job more than his beginning". (Job 42:10-12).

(6) Favour can accelerate the timetable of your assignment and destiny. Joseph became Prime Minister within 24 hours even after suffering for false accusations for years.

(7) One day of favour is worth a lifetime of labour. Ruth was a hardworking peasant. She became rich in a day after she married Boaz.

(8) Favour can stop a tragedy instantly in your life. Favour moved Joseph from prison to Pharaoh's palace in a single day (Gen. 41:39, (40). Esther found favour with the king and saved the entire Jewish nation from extinct.

(9) Anything unrecognized becomes unrewarded and will ultimately exit your life. ☺ What you fail to recognize, you stop celebrating.
    a.   What you stop celebrating, you stop rewarding
    b.   Anything not rewarded will exit your life.

(10) favor will usually cease when not received with thankfulness. Loss is the quickest cure for thankfulness.

(11) Recognition of your dominant source of favour will solve a thousand problems in your life. Stop for a moment.
    1.   Identify the dominant source of favour in your life.
        a. Have you written a note of appreciation?

    b. Have you sown favour to your own family?
    c. Refusing to honour and bless your parents is suicidal. It will destroy you. God guarantees it. Reward your parents for their investments into your life.

(12) You can set the stage for favour to come to you.

APPRECIATE FAVOUR

(1) If you can't appreciate God for the things He has done and is doing, you will depreciate in Him.

(2) Your appreciation of God guarantees your progress.

(3) Your praise guarantees the defeat of your enemies.

(4) If you are not grateful, you will be sorrowful.

(5) Anything not appreciated will leave your life.

(6) Learn to say thank you for favour.

(7) A thank you card or letter, visit or gift is not too much to appreciate favour. It strengthens and encourages one to continue showing you favour.

A tip for an information or assistance is appreciation.

Unusual Favor

And I will grant this people such favor in the sight of the Egyptians that when you leave, you will not go away empty-handed. Exodus 3:21

1. You need people. You need God.

2. You were not designed by God to survive or succeed alone. The earlier you recognize this, the better for you.

3. Everything you have come from God working through people. Success is a collection of relationships. Without Clients, a Lawyer has no career. Without patients, a doctor has no one to cure. Without a writer, a publisher has no business.

4. Your future is connected to people. So develop relationship skills.

5. You need problem-solvers in your life. As you invest into people, people invest into you.

6. You need a family. You need a Pastor to minister to your spiritual needs. You need a doctor for health needs. You need a lawyer for legal matters. You need people who impact your life one way or the other.

7. What is missing in you is in another.

8. Favour will usually come through someone observing you and who is capable of greatly blessing you. It could be your

parents, your boss or your neighbours. It could even be someone you never knew before.

9. Favour is any seed anyone can sow into the life of another. It does not require money, or genius or skill. It requires love, attentiveness and time.

10. Favour should be pursued, requested and celebrated. Abraham's servant in search of a wife for Isaac succeeded because he asked for favour from God. God is the source of favour. He responds to faith and pursuit. Within hours, Rebecca was en-route to Isaac because of the favour of God.

11. Everyone appreciated wants to do more. Everyone appreciated wants to continue the relationship with the appreciator.

12. Look beyond the individual weaknesses and relate within the limits of God's word.

13. Hold unto the relationship as much as it lies within your power. God's instrument of favour may be:
   1. Nameless, powerless, unimportant or insignificant.
   2. Opposed to a close relationship.
   3. Difficult and irritating.
   4. Require you to do something uncomfortable and difficult you have not done before.
   5. Completely the opposite of you.

14. Any relationship that shows favour that is not respected, will exit your life. Cherish relationships. It pays to do that. Build relationships to reap the maximum benefit intended by God who linked you together.

Sow Favour

"Listen! A farmer went out to sow his seed." Mark 4:3

The sower soweth the word... Mark 4:14,26-29

In the morning sow thy seed, and in the evening withhold not thine hand: for thou knowest not whether shall prosper, either this or that, or whether they both *shall be* alike good. Ecclesiastes 11:6

Give ye ear, and hear my voice; hearken, and hear my speech... Isaiah 28:23-26

1. Favor is a seed that anyone can sow into the life of another.

2. Favor always begins when you solve a problem for someone. Joseph interpreted the dream for the butler. Two years later, his gift made room for him in the palace of Pharaoh (Gen. 41:42-44).

3. When others hurt, try to feel it.

4. You are a solution to somebody with a problem. Find them and listen to their cry.

5. You are an influence to someone. Favor is the reward for a good service done.

6. You will only be remembered for the inputs you have made into people's life.

7. Currents of favor always flow when you solve the problem nearest you. When you stop solving problems for others, people stop solving yours.

8. You will begin to succeed in your life when the hurt of others begin to matter to you.

9. Those who unlock your compassion are those to whom you have been assigned.

10. You may not be sent to everyone, but you are definitely sent to someone.

11. The favor of God will meet you at the place where God has sent you.

12. The seed you sow can create the future God has promised you.

13. What you make happen for others, God will make happen for you.

14. God will always cause men to sow into you what you have sown into people's life, same measure, pressed down, shaken together and running over.

15. If you sow a seed of diligence on your job, your harvest will be the favour of promotion.

16. When you sow love into your family, you will reap love. When you sow finances into the work of God, you will reap God's blessings and provision on your finances.

17. Sow favor to reap favor.

18. A sweet and faithful relationship opens the door of favor both from God and man.

19. When a man's ways please the LORD, he makes his enemies to be at peace with him (Prov. 16:7).

20. You can set the stage for favor to come to you.

21. Men shall spend for him that knows how to spend for others.

22. Tithing and giving provoke open heavens. Open heavens are favor.

23. Tomorrows favor is a harvest of the good seeds sown today.

24. You will always reap what you have sown.

25. Sow favor to reap favor Recommend someone.
- Open a door for someone.
- Help someone get a job.
- Stop a lie from being spoken against someone.
- Give money to someone in need.
- Pray for someone.
- Comfort and encourage someone.
- Any other act of kindness that has no selfish interest behind it.

Keys of Favors

Woe to you experts in the law, because you have taken away the key to knowledge. You yourselves have not entered, and you have hindered those who were entering." Luke 11:52

Hold on to instruction, do not let it go; guard it well, for it is your life. Proverbs 4:13

They will be life to your soul and adornment to your neck Proverbs 3:22

He will be the sure foundation for your times, a rich store of salvation and wisdom nd knowledge; the fear of the LORD is the key to this treasure. Isaiah 33:6

1. Favor will stop when you deliberately ignore an instruction from God. When Saul ignored the instructions of Samuel to destroy King Agag, and all the Amalekites, favor stopped. Saul was removed from kingship and David became the King (Sam. 15:9-11, 26).

2. Obedience to God provokes favor (Deut. 28:1-2)

3. Prompt and willing obedience to any and every command of God will bring you into his rest.

4. If a man's ways please the LORD, He will make his enemies to be at peace with him.

5. God's friendship guarantees unlimited favor.

2. The flow of favor is often paralyzed through the development of arrogance and self-sufficiency.

When you no longer recognize God as the source of your blessing, you automatically slam the door against yourself. When Nebuchadnezzar sneered at the authority of God because of his success, God permitted him to live a beast in the field until his humility returned (Daniel 5:20, 21).

3. The river of favor will dry up when God observed greed.

"Will man rob God? Yet ye have robbed me. But ye say, wherein have we robbed thee? In tithes and offerings. Ye are cursed with a curse: for ye have robbed me, even this whole nation". (Malachi 3:8, 9).

It is tragedy, an absurdity and futility to try to breathe favor into a family or a man whom God has chosen to discipline (curse) because of their greed.

4. Lack of forgiveness and bitterness of heart stops the flow of favor. When you refuse to forgive the one who has offended you, God will not forgive you. And he cannot favor you when he has not forgiven you.

"For if you forgive men when they sin against you, your heavenly Father will also forgive you. But if you do not forgive men their sins, your Father will not forgive your sins" (Matthew 6:14,15).

"...Forgiving each other, just as in Christ God forgave you" (Ephesians 4:32).

Forgive, as you are offended, and keep the door of blessing open.

Expect Favour

For let not that man think that he shall receive any thing of the Lord. James 1:7

But he must ask in faith, without doubting, because he who doubts is like a wave of the sea, blown and tossed by the wind.

James 1:6
"Truly I tell you that if anyone says to this mountain, 'Be lifted up and thrown into the sea,' and has no doubt in his heart but believes that it will happen, it will be done for him.

Mark 11:23
Get up! Go downstairs and accompany them without hesitation, because I have sent them."

Acts 10:20
An understanding of the Law of sowing and reaping and all that have been taught so far does not leave you in doubt that you have to be expectant. We live on the favor of God manifested through man. As we walk with God in faithful obedience, He favors us.

1. Expectation makes one to recognize the fact that no matter how skillful or educated a man may be, he needs the supernatural power of God to assist him.

"Trust in the LORD with all your heart and lean not on your own understanding; in all your ways acknowledge Him, and He will make your paths straight" (Prov. 3:5, 6).

"The race is not to the swift or the battle to the strong, nor does food come to the wise or wealth to the brilliant or favor to the learned; but time and chance happen to them all" (Eccl. 9:1).

Time and chance are the supernatural touch to everything that happens in man's life.
2. Expectation is a reflection of faith in the love of God.
3. Expectation is a proof that one is ready to receive.
4. Expectation is an indication that one will give glory to God when the expected is done. Sow favor and expect favor to be sown back into your own life. Walk with God and He will favor you all the way. He will never abandon you.

Happened was that the favor of God on Nehemiah attracted people to him. Other people wanted to connect with Nehemiah and be a part of his mission! This is exactly what the favor of God can do for you and me, today too!

Nehemiah walked in God's favor and it brought such boldness in the hearts of other people also that when there was opposition, all of them responded to the opposition saying, "The God of heaven, He will prosper us.

Therefore we, his servants, will arise and build" (Nehemiah 2:20). Thus, they knew they were in a season of divine favor and recognized what God was doing in their midst. They believed that the good hand of God's favor was upon them, and no matter what people said, they were going to rise up and build.

Genesis 39 records the story of Joseph being sold by his brothers as a slave to Egypt. There he served in Potiphar's house and was later thrown into prison.

FAVOR will bless the righteous. He will surround them with favor like a shield. So when we are walking in righteousness, we are surrounded with divine favor. So no matter whoever comes into contact with us, they will come into contact with this invisible favor—a shield of favor.

Let love and faithfulness never leave you; bind them around your neck, write them on the tablet of your heart. 4 Then you will win favor and a good name in the sight of God and man. (Proverbs 3:3,4).

Good people obtain favor from the Lord, but he condemns those who devise wicked schemes. (Proverbs 12:2).

There are two things that God really wants us to keep in our hearts—'Mercy' which is compassion, and 'Truth' which is integrity, uprightness and honesty. God says that if we maintain these two things, we find favor in high esteem before God and before man. So what actually attracts favor to our lives is when we are walking with mercy and truth.

For those who find me find life and receive favor from the Lord (Proverbs 8:35).

Benefits of God's favor

Bless the LORD, O my soul, and forget not all his benefits:
Psalm 103:2

Deuteronomy 6:12 be careful not to forget the LORD who brought you out of the land of Egypt, out of the house of slavery.

Be careful not to forget the LORD your God by failing to keep His commandments and ordinances and statutes, which I am giving you this day.

Deuteronomy 8:11
Remember the wonders He has done, His marvels, and the judgments He has pronounced, 1 Chronicles 16:12

How can I repay the LORD for all His goodness to me?

Psalm 116:12
And declared: "Blessed be the name of God forever and ever, for wisdom and power belong to Him. Daniel 2:20

This prayer is only a guideline. You can also pray in your own words.

Dear Lord Jesus, today, I have understood what You did for me on the cross.

You died for me, you shed Your precious blood and paid the penalty for my sins, so that I could be forgiven.

The Bible tells me that whoever believes in You will receive forgiveness for their sins.

Today, I make a decision to believe in You and to accept what You did for me, by dying for me on the cross and rising again from the dead.

I know I cannot save myself by my own good works, neither can any other human save me. I cannot earn forgiveness for my sins.

Today, I believe in my heart and say with my mouth that You died for me, You paid the penalty for my sins, You rose again from the dead, and by faith in You, I receive forgiveness and cleansing for my sins..

Thank You Jesus. Help me to love You, to know You more.

1)   Favor produces supernatural increase and promotion Genesis 39:21

2)   Favor produces restoration of everything that the enemy has stolen from you. Exodus 3:21

3)   Favor produces honor in the midst of your adversaries. Exodus 11:3

4)   Favor produces increased assets, especially in the area of real estate. Deuteronomy 33:23

5)   Favor produces great victories in the midst of great impossibilities. Joshua 11:20

6) Favor produces recognition, even when you seem the least likely to receive it. I Samuel 16:22

7) Favor produces prominence and preferential treatment. Esther 2:17

8) Favor produces petitions granted even by ungodly civil authorities. Esther 5:8

9) Favor causes policies, rules, regulations and laws to be changed and reversed to your advantage. Esther 8:5

10) Favor produces battles won which you won't even fight because God will fight them for you. Psalm 44:3

11) The Lord helps me to guard the door of my mouth and trains me not to speak against His favor at work in my life (Psalm 141:3, AMP).

12) I will not allow any corrupt communication to proceed out of my mouth. Instead, I will speak only that which is good, full of grace and edifying to others (Ephesians 4:29).

13) As the righteousness of God, I declare that I am highly favored in God's sight (Job 33:26, AMP; Psalm 5:12; Proverbs 14:9).

14) Like Joseph, I prosper in every place and in every situation I am in, because the Lord is always with me. I, too, experience preferential treatment (Genesis 39:1-6, 21).

15) I am blessed and highly favored (Luke 1:28).

16) I associate with those who are blessed and highly favored so that I may increase in every area of my life (Genesis 30:27).

17) I operate in integrity; as a result, I obtain favor from God (Proverbs 11:27; Proverbs 12:2).

18) I actively seek and live by God's wisdom; therefore, I am highly favored and esteemed in the sight of God and men (Proverbs 3:1-4; Proverbs 8:33-35).

19) God's favor brings promotion and causes me to increase daily (Esther 2:17; Psalm 75:6-7).

20) The Lord takes pleasure in my prosperity. He desires for me to prosper in every area of my life--spiritually, financially, emotionally, physically, mentally and socially (Psalm 35:27; 3 John 2).

21) The favor of God shields me; therefore, no sickness or disease can live in my body (Deuteronomy 7:15; Psalm 5:12).

22) Wealth and riches are in my house because I am empowered with God's anointing and favor to draw wealth (Deuteronomy 8:18; Psalm 112:3).

23) God is pleased with me and His favor endures for a lifetime (Psalm 30:5, AMP).

24) God surrounds and protects me with favor like a shield (Psalm 5:12).

25) Fear cannot rule in my life because I have favor with God (Luke 1:30).

26) My enemies cannot triumph over me because the Lord has favored me (Psalm 41:11).

Joseph's Life

Then Midianite traders passed by; so the brothers pulled Joseph up and lifted him out of the pit, and sold him to the Ishmaelites for twenty shekels of silver. And they took Joseph to Egypt. Genesis 37:28

Because the patriarchs were jealous of Joseph, they sold him as a slave into Egypt. But God was with him Acts 7:9

And as they sat down to eat a meal, they looked up and saw a caravan of Ishmaelites coming from Gilead. Their camels were carrying spices, balm, and myrrh on their way down to Egypt. Genesis 37:25

Meanwhile, Joseph had been taken down to Egypt, where an Egyptian named Potiphar, an officer of Pharaoh and captain of the guard, bought him from the Ishmaelites who had taken him there. Genesis 39:1

Then Joseph said to his brothers, "Please come near me." And they did so. "I am Joseph, your brother," he said, "the one you sold into Egypt! Genesis 45:4

And ow, do not be distressed or angry with yourselves that you sold me into this place, because it was to save lives that God sent me before you.

Genesis 45:5
The life of Joseph is a great study on God's favor and success. His story is a classic example of how someone can face

unbelievable rejection and setbacks and still come out on top with God's favor. I'm sure you remember the story.

As a young boy, Joseph was sold by his own brothers into slavery (Gen 37). Can you imagine the horrible rejection and hurt that an event like that could produce? I'm sure that Joseph was tempted to be bitter just like anyone would. Yet, when you read the whole story, there's no mention of bitterness or a desire for revenge. In fact, it's quite the opposite. Joseph seems to have risen above the hurt through His faith in God's destiny for his life.

The Bible says that when his brothers sold him, the slave traders put him in chains and took him down to Egypt (Gen 39 / Ps 105:17-22). There, he was sold again and ended up in Potiphar's house. At that horrible time in his life, look at what Genesis 39:2-4 says about Joseph: "And the Lord was with Joseph, and he was a prosperous man; and he was in the house of his master the Egyptian. And his master saw that the Lord was with him and that the Lord made all that he did to prosper in his hand.

And Joseph found FAVOR in his sight, and he served him; and he made him overseer over his house and all that he had put into his hand." Keep in mind that this was said of Joseph when he was a slave and owned absolutely nothing. Prosperous? Favor? This one passage alone confirms that God's view of prosperity and success is far different than the world's view. In God's mind, "prosperity" is all about who you are on the inside, not what you have on the outside. God looked upon Joseph's faith and attitude and called him "prosperous." And because he was prosperous on the inside, it was just a matter of time until he experienced God's favor and blessing on the outside. Never forget that prosperity is first and foremost who you are on the inside.

In the Name of Jesus, I decree from this moment forward, I see myself the way God sees me. I am highly favored of the Lord. I am crowned with glory and honor. I am the righteousness of God in Christ and reigning as a King in life through the one man Jesus Christ the Messiah.

In Jesus' Name, I declare by faith that I walk in divine favor. I have preferential treatment, supernatural increase, restoration, increased assets, great victories, recognition, prominence, petitions granted, policies and rules changed and battles won I do not have to fight, all because of the Blessing and favor of God on my life.

In Jesus' Name, every morning when I arise, I expect divine favor to go before me and surround me as with a shield with good will and pleasures forevermore. Doors are now open for me that men say are impossible to open. No obstacle can stop me, and no hindrances can delay me.

In Jesus' Name, I am honored by my Father, as I receive genuine favor that comes directly from Him. I am special to Him. I am the object of His affection. I am blessed and highly favored of the Lord, in Jesus' Name. Amen.

Power of Favor

God's favor was activated and Joseph was made the overseer of the prison (Gen 39:21-23). The account says that the Lord was "with" Joseph / that he found "favor" / and that the Lord "made him" to prosper. What an amazing story of favor! When we examine Joseph's life (and include insights from the New Testament), there are a number of favor-keys that we can discover. These keys will help you better understand how to experience God's favor in your own life, first and foremost who you are on the "inside" (in your mind, heart, and character) and not what you have on the outside. God already sees you as a winner.

1)   If you are a prosperous person on the inside then it's just be a matter of time until you will see things change on the outside (if you refuse to give up). Hold on to your faith.

2)   The experiential side of God's favor is linked to how you respond to adversities, setbacks, offenses, and temptations. Keep trusting God.

3)   The principle of "working as unto the Lord" activates God's favor and blessing. It's the way you can express your faith each and every day regardless of what kind of work you do.

4)   believing in and expecting continual supernatural moves of God in your daily life.

5)   doing what you say you're going to do. . .when you say you're going to do it.

6)   Being a person of integrity even when no one else is around.

7)   Being a person of character instead of being a character.

8)   Live an Ephesians 6:8 lifestyle.

9)   Treat people the way you want to be treated.
10) Position yourself for His favor to flow through you to others.

1.   Praising God will give you favor.

If you want to know how to move in God's supernatural favor. . .you'll find an amazing answer in Acts 2:47 which says:
"Praising God, and having favour with all the people. And the Lord added to the church daily such as should be saved."
According to Strong's Concordance the Greek word for praising is aineō (G134) and it means: "to praise, extol, to sing praises in honour to God; to allow, recommend; to promise or vow"
Praising comes from the Greek root word ainos (G136) which means: "a saying, proverb; praise, laudatory discourse."
When you begin to praise God. . .you change the spiritual atmosphere. . .wherever you are and whatever you're going through.
If you feel like the hordes of hell have carpooled and headed to your house. . .then just start praising God for what He's done and is doing in your life.
Start with the basics. . .thank God for being able to breathe on your own. . .to hear others speak and being able to speak so others hear you. When words of praise start flowing from your lips. . .circumstances change. . .adversaries flee. . .thoughts are purified and energized by the Holy Spirit. . .which leaves a spiritual confidence. . .with every person you meet.

2.   When you accept a difficult assignment you move in His favor.

If God knew you before you were formed in your mother's womb and He does... don't you think He knows every situation and circumstance you will face on your journey through this earth?

Luke 1:29-31 in the Amplified Bible says:

"But when she saw him, she was greatly troubled and disturbed and confused at what he said and kept revolving in her mind what such a greeting might mean.

"And the angel said to her, Do not be afraid, Mary, for you have found grace (free, spontaneous, absolute favor and loving-kindness) with God.

"And listen! You will become pregnant and will give birth to a Son, and you shall call His name Jesus."

Why do you think Mary found "absolute favor" with God. . .could it be because He knew her character well enough to know how she'd respond?

Luke 1:34-35, 37-38 says: "Then said Mary unto the angel, How shall this be, seeing I know not a man?

And the angel answered and said unto her, The Holy Ghost shall come upon thee, and the power of the Highest shall overshadow thee: therefore also that holy thing which shall be born of thee shall be called the Son of God. . .For with God nothing shall be impossible. And Mary said, Behold the handmaid of the Lord; be it unto me according to thy word. And the angel departed from her."

Mary knew she had never been with a man. . .so asking "how shall this be"was a logical question. But . . . she didn't say, "This can't happen. . .it's never been done before." Her question was not one of doubt but of inquiry. She knew there was something about to happen. . .that she'd never experienced before. Something beyond the natural realm . . . something born of the spirit.

40

God counted on Mary being obedient. . .when it wasn't convenient.God knew within Mary's heart she could agree to do something. . . where her actions would be misunderstood and slandered. . .even at the risk of her own death.

Why do you think. . .the people didn't stone Mary to death as the law directed. . .it's because she was moving in the favor of God.

Five verses before the angel reveals Mary's future to her. . .she is referred to as "highly favoured."

Luke 1:28 says: "And the angel came in unto her, and said, Hail, thou that art highly favoured, the Lord is with thee: blessed art thou among women."

Like Mary. . .you may be facing seemingly impossible circumstances or problems. . .but if you respond. . .despite the severity of the adversity. . .as simply as. . . "be it according to you Word". . .then you too. . .will be moving in supernatural favor.

3.   When you increase in wisdom. . .you increase in favor with God.

Luke 2:52 says: "And Jesus increased in wisdom and stature, and in favour with God and man." According to Strong's Concordance wisdom is the Greek word sophia (G4678) and it means: "wisdom, broad and full of intelligence; the wisdom which belongs to men

1) the varied knowledge of things human and divine, acquired by acuteness and experience, and summed up in saws and proverbs

2) the science and learning

3) the act of interpreting dreams and always giving the sagest advice

4) the intelligence evidenced in discovering the meaning of some mysterious number or vision

5) skill in the management of affairs

6) devout and proper prudence in intercourse with men not disciples of Christ, skill and discretion in imparting Christian truth

7) the knowledge and practice of the requisites for godly and upright living"

It's the same Greek word found in Luke 21:15 in the Amplified Bible which says:

"For I [Myself] will give you a mouth and such utterance and wisdom that all of your foes combined will be unable to stand against or refute."

It's also used in 1 Corinthians 1:24 in the Amplified Bible which says:

"But to those who are called, whether Jew or Greek (Gentile), Christ [is] the Power of God and the Wisdom of God."

How do you and I get this wisdom? James 1:5 says:

"If any of you lack wisdom, let him ask of God, that giveth to all men liberally, and upbraideth not; and it shall be given him."

Luke 2:52 makes it clear to me. . .there is an proportionate increase in favour as you increase in wisdom. Once again the verse says:

"And Jesus increased in wisdom and stature, and in favour with God and man."

If you want to walk in supernatural favor. . .get wisdom.

4. His irresistible charm will flow through you to other people.

Even in the midst of difficult circumstances. . .the supernatural favor of God will flow through you.

Genesis 39:21 says:

"But the Lord was with Joseph, and shewed him mercy, and gave him favour in the sight of the keeper of the prison."

While most believers will never find themselves confined in a prison with guards and tungsten steel wire fences. . .they may feel incarcerated by their surroundings. . .feeling that freedom. . .financial and otherwise. . .is just an elusive dream.

No matter what circumstances you're facing. . .God can move you from the prison to the palace. . .as His irresistible charm flows through you to change hearts and attitudes toward you.

Acts 7:10 in the Amplified Bible says:

"And delivered him from all his distressing afflictions and won him goodwill and favor and wisdom and understanding in the sight of Pharaoh, king of Egypt, who made him governor over Egypt and all his house."

God will even give you favor with people who have tortured you. . .laughed at you. . .perhaps even enslaved you.

Exodus 12:36 in the Amplified Bible says:

"The Lord gave the people favor in the sight of the Egyptians, so that they gave them what they asked. And they stripped the Egyptians [of those things]."

God's WORD Translation of Exodus 12:36 says: ". . .So the Israelites stripped Egypt of its wealth."

So my prayer is for the irresistible charm of Jesus to flow through you. . .giving you favor with every person you meet. Many of these people may not even know why they're giving you such favor. . .but we will know.

We will know.

5. Never leave home without it.

Years ago, American Express had an ad campaign which suggested we "Never leave home without their credit card."

a long time ago, I used to say . .we were so broke. . .American Express wrote me a letter and said "Please leave home without it." Not really, just a little humor.

1 Corinthians 16:23 in the Amplified Bible says:

"The grace (favor and spiritual blessing) of our Lord Jesus Christ be with you."

From the time we awakened in the morning till we pillow our heads at night. . .our Heavenly Father wants us talking, walking, living and acting in His favor. . .wherever we go and in whatever we're doing. . .as long as. . .we bring glory and honor to Him.

Oftentimes we don't walk in favour because we don't ask for it or expect it.

Do you expect to find a parking space close to the entrance of the mall? When you do. . .that's the favour of God.

For a number of years, my fine wife Bev taught a wonderful group of high school and college girls. She taught them to always pray for favor in everything even including parking spots wherever they went.

One of the students returned to the campus one Sunday praying as usual for favor in finding a parking spot close to her dorm at East Carolina University but there was not one to me found.

The student was disappointed at having to park on the other side of the campus until the next morning when the light of day revealed that the severe thunderstorm that came through during the night have blown rocks off the top of her dorm damaging all the cars that had parked close.

There will be moments where we pray for favor in specific situations thinking that things should go one way. . .when, in fact, something else is better. But whatever the scenario we've got must realize that "Father Knows Best" and I'm not talking about the old TV show.

Psalm 139:5 in the Message Bible says:

"You know when I leave and when I get back; I'm never out of your sight. You know everything I'm going to say before I start the first sentence.

"I look behind me and you're there, then up ahead and you're there, too—your reassuring presence, coming and going. This is too much, too wonderful—I can't take it all in!"

6.   Even sinners recognize the favor of God on you.

"I don't know what it is but things always seem to go your way."

It's important for each of to realize that even when the enemy tries to trip us up. . .or traps for us. . .he loses and we ALWAYS win.

Take comfort in Proverbs 12:13 in the Amplified Bible which says:

"The wicked is [dangerously] snared by the transgression of his lips, but the [uncompromisingly] righteous shall come out of trouble."

Not only come out of trouble. . .but many times. . .the favour of God will keep us from ever falling into traps of the enemy.

Psalm 91:3 in the Contemporary English Version says:

"The Lord will keep you safe from secret traps and deadly diseases."

Jacob had his wages changed ten times by his conniving and greedy father-in-law Laban. Despite the best efforts of a sinful man. . .Jacob continued to prosper because Jacob kept his trust in God.

The favor of God on Jacob. . .became clearly evident to Laban.

Genesis 30:27 says:

"And Laban said unto him, I pray thee, if I have found favour in thine eyes, tarry: for I have learned by experience that the Lord hath blessed me for thy sake."

Even sinners can't overlook, deny or rationalize away the supernatural favor on God on someone's life.

Genesis 21:22 in the New Living Translation says:

"About this time, Abimelech came with Phicol, his army commander, to visit Abraham. "God is obviously with you, helping you in everything you do," Abimelech said."

What a witness. . .for God's favor on your life to be clearly evident to everyone around you.

7.   Double favor can be yours.

2 Corinthians 1:15 in the Amplified Bible says:

"It was with assurance of this that I wanted and planned to visit you first [of all], so that you might have a double favor and token of grace (goodwill)."

The New Living Translation of 2 Corinthians 1:15 says:

"Since I was so sure of your understanding and trust, I wanted to give you a double blessing by visiting you twice."

Talk about favor. . .two visits by Paul would be an incredible experience. The opportunity of being in his presence. . .experiencing the power flowing through him and the revelation pouring out of him.

What would put a person in such a unique position? Simply put, obeying what the word says whether it's convenient or not. Doing what God says we should be doing and how we should be doing it.

LAW OF FAVOR

GOD GIVE US DIVINE FAVOR; IT IS YOUR BIRTHRIGHT. EXPECT FAVOR IN YOUR LIFE LIKE JESUS HAD ON HIS LIFE. PSALMS 102:13, 16

• FAVOR AND GRACE ARE INTERCHANGEABLE. FAVOR CAN INCREASE IN YOUR LIFE. LUKE 2:40, 52; LUKE 1:28

• FAITH IS STILL A REQUIREMENT TO RECEIVE FAVOR. FAVOR DOES NOT GUARANTEE FREEDOM FROM PROBLEMS. I SAMUEL 16:7, GENESIS 37:3, 5-10

• GOD WILL BLESS YOU WITH AN ABUNDANCE OF FAVOR. FAVOR WILL OPEN DOORS FOR YOU THAT YOU CANNOT OPEN. GENESIS 12:1-3 (KJV/AMP), GALATIANS 3:9, 13-14, 29

• AS LONG AS YOU ARE IN THE KINGDOM OF GOD AND HAVE HIS FAVOR, YOU CANNOT BE DEFEATED. GENESIS 39:2, 4-6; JOHN 15:5, PSALM 30:4-5

• THE DEVIL HAS OCCUPIED THE KINGDOMS OF THIS WORLD AND TRIED TO TEMPT JESUS TO WORSHIP HIM. LUKE 4:1-5

•The 7 pillars (Kingdoms) – religion, family, education, government, media, arts & entertainment (sports), and business. Luke 4:1-5, revelation 11:15

•God has planted you as a seed in a specific sphere in order to take over and take back what rightfully belongs to those in the kingdom of god.   Proverbs 9:1

• FAVOR DOES NOT GUARANTEE FREEDOM FROM PROBLEMS. GENESIS 37:3, 8-10; 5-10

• GOD DELIBERATELY PLANTS THE RIGHTEOUS AMONG THE WICKED TO BE A BLESSING. THE DEVIL IS AFTER THE VISION, BLESSING AND FAVOR THAT IS ON THOSE IN THE KINGDOM OF GOD. GENESIS 39:2, 4-6, 21; JOHN 17:15; GENESIS 12:1-3 (KJV/AMP)

• SATAN HAS ASSIGNED DEMONIC SPIRITS TO SPECIFIC SPHERES. WE ARE SENT TO LIFT THE CURSE OFF WHERE EVER WE ARE.   DANIEL 1:9, I JOHN 5:19, EPHESIANS 6:11-12

• THE CHURCH IS IN CHARGE OF THE KINGDOM. PRAYER WILL CONNECT YOU WITH THE POWER OF GOD. DANIEL 6:10, 10:12-14, 20; 2 CORINTHIANS 4:3-4

Understanding Favor

Favor is a gift from God that you can't work for; it is to be a blessing and not revenge.

Favor: regard with kindness, give aid, give prominence, give support, wish success to, afford special advantages, show special privileges, endorse, make easier, give unfair partiality, grant preferential treatment.

Favor determines your destiny.   psalm 102:13, 16; I Samuel 16:7

When you have favor or grace on your life, nothing can stop you. expect to win.   I Corinthians 15:10, Luke 2:52, Luke 4:18-19 (KJV/AMP),   Matthew 27:12-14, 19

Favor will make you a blessing where you will be able to distribute to others.   genesis 12:1-2 (KJV/AMP), genesis 24:1 (kjv/amp); genesis 24:35

Favor promised to Abraham is also promised to you; you have to learn how to walk in favor.
     galatians 3:7, 9, 13-14, 29

One encounter with favor is worth a lifetime of labor.   Exodus 3:19

Favor is life; decree favor over yourself.   psalm 30:5, genesis 39:6, 9, 21-23; job 22:8

Favor opens doors for you; Faith is positive, it sees the invisible. genesis 40:7, 14

You have been called to solve problems; you have been chosen by god. Expect favor and decree it.   Ephesians 1:4, job 22:28

When you have favor, you are divinely positioned. Pray favor over your family for protection. I Samuel 16:6; 8:19; 9:2

Increase of favor

1. F FAITH, FEAR AND FAITHFULNESS
2. A ACCURATE EXEGESIS
3. V VIRTUOUS MEDITATION
4. O OBEDIENCE
5. U UNITY
6. R RIGHTEOUSNESS
7. I ILLUMINATION(WISDOM)
8. T THANKSGIVING
9. E EXCELLENCE
10. S SACRIFICE

1. FAITH, FEAR AND FAITHFULNESS

1.1 FAITH

Hebrews 11:5-6 AMP (5) Because of faith Enoch was caught up and transferred to heaven, so that he did not have a glimpse of death; and he was not found, because God had translated him. For even before he was taken to heaven, he received testimony [still on record] that he had pleased and been satisfactory to God.

[Genesis 5:21-24] (6) But without faith it is impossible to please and be satisfactory to Him. For whoever would come near to God must [necessarily] believe that God exists and that He is the rewarder of those who earnestly and diligently seek Him [out].

1.2. FEAR OF GOD

Psalms 147:11 AMP The Lord takes pleasure in those who reverently and worshipfully fear Him, in those who hope in His mercy and loving-kindness. [Psalms 145:20]

Luke 1:50 AMP And His mercy (His compassion and kindness toward the miserable and afflicted) is on those who fear Him with godly reverence, from generation to generation and age to age. [Psalms 103:17]

Psalms 33:18-19 AMP (18) Behold, the Lord's eye is upon those who fear Him [who revere and worship Him with awe], who wait for Him and hope in His mercy and lovingkindness, (19) To deliver them from death and keep them alive in famine.

1.3. FAITHFULNESS

Proverbs 28:20 AMP A faithful man shall abound with blessings, but he who makes haste to be rich [at any cost] shall not go unpunished. [Proverbs 13:11; 20:21; 23:4; 1 Timothy 6:9]

1 Samuel 22:14 AMP Then Ahimelech answered the king, And who is so faithful among all your servants as David, who is the king's son-in-law, and is taken into your council and honored in your house?

Psalms 101:6 AMP My eyes shall [look with favor] upon the faithful of the land, that they may dwell with me; he who walks blamelessly, he shall minister to me.

Luke 12:42-44 AMP (42) And the Lord said, Who then is that faithful steward, the wise man whom his master will set over those in his household service to supply them their allowance of food at the appointed time? (43) Blessed (happy and to be envied) is that servant whom his master finds so doing when he arrives. (44) Truly I tell you, he will set him in charge over all his possessions.

Daniel 6:3-5 AMP (3) Then this Daniel was distinguished above the presidents and the satraps because an excellent spirit was in him, and the king thought to set him over the whole realm. (4) Then the presidents and satraps sought to find occasion [to bring accusation] against Daniel concerning the kingdom, but they could find no occasion or fault, for he was faithful, nor was there any error or fault found in him. (5) Then said these men, We shall not find any occasion [to bring accusation] against this Daniel except we find it against him concerning the law of his God. [Acts 24:13-21; 1 Peter 4:12-16]

2. ACCURATE EXEGESIS

2 Timothy 2:15 AMP Study and be eager and do your utmost to present yourself to God approved (tested by trial), a workman who has no cause to be ashamed, correctly analyzing and accurately dividing [rightly handling and skillfully teaching] the Word of Truth.

Isaiah 28:9-12 AMP (9) To whom will He teach knowledge? [Ask the drunkards] And whom will He make to understand the message? Those who are babies, just weaned from the milk and taken from the breasts? [Is that what He thinks we are?]
(10) For it is [His prophets repeating over and over]: precept upon precept, precept upon precept, rule upon rule, rule upon rule; here a little, there a little. (11) No, but [the Lord will teach the rebels in a more humiliating way] by men with stammering lips and another tongue will He speak to this people [says Isaiah, and teach them His lessons]. (12) To these [complaining

Jews the Lord] had said, This is the true rest [the way to true comfort and happiness] that you shall give to the weary, and, This is the [true] refreshing--yet they would not listen [to His teaching].

3. VIRTUOUS MEDITATION

Psalms 119:70 AMP Their hearts are as fat as grease [their minds are dull and brutal], but I delight in Your law.

Psalms 40:8 AMP I delight to do Your will, O my God; yes, Your law is within my heart. [Hebrews 10:5-9]

Jeremiah 15:16 AMP Your words were found, and I ate them; and Your words were to me a joy and the rejoicing of my heart, for I am called by Your name, O Lord God of hosts.

Romans 7:22 AMP For I endorse and delight in the Law of God in my inmost self [with my new nature]. [Psalms 1:2]

Psalms 37:4 AMP Delight yourself also in the Lord, and He will give you the desires and secret petitions of your heart.

THE END-RESULT OF VIRTUOUS MEDITATION IS FAVOUR – vs.3

Psalms 1:2-3 AMP (2) But his delight and desire are in the law of the Lord, and on His law (the precepts, the instructions, the teachings of God) he habitually meditates (ponders and studies) by day and by night. [Romans 13:8-10; Galatians 3:1-29; 2 Timothy 3:16] (3) And he shall be like a tree firmly planted [and tended] by the streams of water, ready to bring forth its fruit in its season; its leaf also shall not fade or wither;

and everything he does shall prosper [and come to maturity].
[Jeremiah 17:7, 8]

The Result is Favor

THE PSALMIST DECLARES HIS PASSION FOR THE WORD – DEMONSTRATED IN HIS PURSUIT AND MEDITATION. THE END RESULT IS FAVOUR AS SEEN IN VS. 65.

Psalms 119:40-65 AMP

(40) Behold, I long for Your precepts; in Your righteousness give me renewed life.

(41) Let Your mercy and loving-kindness come also to me, O Lord, even Your salvation according to Your promise;

(42) Then shall I have an answer for those who taunt and reproach me, for I lean on, rely on, and trust in Your word.

(43) And take not the word of truth utterly out of my mouth, for I hope in Your ordinances.

(44) I will keep Your law continually, forever and ever [hearing, receiving, loving, and obeying it].

(45) And I will walk at liberty and at ease, for I have sought and inquired for [and desperately required] Your precepts.

(46) I will speak of Your testimonies also before kings and will not be put to shame. [Psalms 138:1; Matthew 10:18, 19; Acts 26:1, 2]

(47) For I will delight myself in Your commandments, which I love.

(48) My hands also will I lift up [in fervent supplication] to Your commandments, which I love, and I will meditate on Your statutes.

(49) Remember [fervently] the word and promise to Your servant, in which You have caused me to hope.

(50) This is my comfort and consolation in my affliction: that Your word has revived me and given me life. [Romans 15:4]

(51) The proud have had me greatly in derision, yet have I not declined in my interest in or turned aside from Your law.

(52) When I have [earnestly] recalled Your ordinances from of old, O Lord, I have taken comfort.

(53) Burning indignation, terror, and sadness seize upon me because of the wicked, who forsake Your law. (54) Your statutes have been my songs in the house of my pilgrimage.

(55) I have [earnestly] remembered Your name, O Lord, in the night, and I have observed Your law.

(56) This I have had [as the gift of Your grace and as my reward]: that I have kept Your precepts [hearing, receiving, loving, and obeying them].

(57) You are my portion, O Lord; I have promised to keep Your words.

(58) I entreated Your favor with my whole heart; be merciful and gracious to me according to Your promise.

(59) I considered my ways; I turned my feet to [obey] Your testimonies.

(60) I made haste and delayed not to keep Your commandments.

(61) Though the cords of the wicked have enclosed and ensnared me, I have not forgotten Your law.

(62) At midnight I will rise to give thanks to You because of Your righteous ordinances.

(63) I am a companion of all those who fear, revere, and worship You, and of those who observe and give heed to Your precepts.

(64) The earth, O Lord, is full of Your mercy and loving-kindness; teach me Your statutes.

(65) You have dealt well with Your servant, O Lord, according to Your promise.

Favor in Obedience

(precepts, promise, laws, word, ordinances, righteous judgements, commandments – all refer to the WORD.)

OBEDIENCE

1. OBEDIENCE TO PARENTS

Colossians 3:20 AMP Children, obey your parents in everything, for this is pleasing to the Lord.

2. OBEYING GOD

1 Samuel 15:22 AMP Samuel said, Has the Lord as great a delight in burnt offerings and sacrifices as in obeying the voice of the Lord? Behold, to obey is better than sacrifice, and to hearken than the fat of rams.

All great men in the Bible were great because they obeyed God.
• Abraham obeyed God when God asked him to sacrifice his son Isaac.
• Noah obeyed God in building the Ark.
• Lot obeyed God in leaving the city.
• Mary obeyed God in allowing herself to be a vessel to deliver the Messiah.

Obedience is better than sacrifice. Often it is easier to sacrifice than to obey. People often find it easier to fast and tithe than to obey two of Jesus's basic commandments, namely:

1. Love one another (John 13:34).

2. Make disciples (Matt.28:19-20).

Deuteronomy 15:5-6 AMP (5) If only you carefully listen to the voice of the Lord your God, to do watchfully all these commandments which I command you this day. (6) When the Lord your God blesses you as He promised you, then you shall lend to many nations, but you shall not borrow; and you shall rule over many nations, but they shall not rule over you.

Deuteronomy 30:10-16 AMP (10) If you obey the voice of the Lord your God, to keep His commandments and His statutes which are written in this Book of the Law, and if you turn to the Lord your God with all your [mind and] heart and with all your being. (11) For this commandment which I command you this day is not too difficult for you, nor is it far off. (12) It is not [a secret laid up] in heaven, that you should say, Who shall go up for us to heaven and bring it to us, that we may hear and do it? (13) Neither is it beyond the sea, that you should say, Who shall go over the sea for us and bring it to us, that we may hear and do it?

(14) But the word is very near you, in your mouth and in your mind and in your heart, so that you can do it. (15) See, I have set before you this day life and good, and death and evil. (16) [If you obey the commandments of the Lord your God which] I command you today, to love the Lord your God, to walk in His ways, and to keep His commandments and His statutes and His ordinances, then you shall live and multiply, and the Lord your God will bless you in the land into which you go to possess.

Jeremiah 7:23 AMP But this thing I did command them: Listen to and obey My voice, and I will be your God and you will be My people; and walk in the whole way that I command you, that it may be well with you.

3. UNITY / ONENESS

Ephesians 4:3 AMP Be eager and strive earnestly to guard and keep the harmony and oneness of [and produced by] the Spirit in the binding power of peace.

Jesus prayed that we may be one.

This word oneness has been translated in m any of the versions of the Bible as being unity. I believe that the word unity cannot fully describe the concept of oneness. You can be in unity and still not be of one mind. You can agree to disagree and still have a unity of heart.

Unity is all about us coming to a place of agreement about something. You will find that unity speaks of being in agreement and in harmony.

Oneness speaks of a dimension of unity that goes much further. It speaks of coming to a place and position where we become one unit. We think the same our doctrine is the same. The best way to put it is where we become one with the Lord and one another.

Again my favourite scripture of 1 John 2:29 comes to mind.

It is the place where all of us that are oneO.. are aligned to the will of the Father in our thoughts, purpose and our actions.

1 John 2:29 AMP If you know (perceive and are sure) that He [Christ] is [absolutely] righteous [conforming to the Father's

will in purpose, thought, and action], you may also know (be sure) that everyone who does righteously [and is therefore in like manner conformed to the divine will] is born (begotten) of Him [God].

This is where God demands his FAVOUR to be released.

John 17:21 AMP That they all may be one, [just] as You, Father, are in Me and I in You, that they also may be one in Us, so that the world may believe and be convinced that You have sent Me.

In His prayer Jesus is not praying for unity and agreement. His prayer is for oneness. Being one as the trinity is one.

Psalms 133:1-3 AMP

(1)   Behold, how good and how pleasant it is for brethren to dwell together in unity!

(2)   It is like the precious ointment poured on the head, that ran down on the beard, even the beard of Aaron [the first high priest], that came down upon the collar and skirts of his garments [consecrating the whole body]. [Exodus 30:25, 30]

(3)   It is like the dew of [lofty] Mount Hermon and the dew that comes on the hills of Zion; for there the Lord has commanded the blessing, even life forevermore [upon the high and the lowly].

Opportunity in Favor

The Purpose of This book Few people ever learn how to walk in the favor of God. Others have been walking in His favor for years and did not recognize it. In this series we will learn how to identify activate the key components that attracts the favor of God and the favor of man toward our life as a believer. Too few have enjoyed the rich blessings that God has for each of His children, it's time we engage in this open opportunity to find favor! The Purpose of This Message: Todays message is to open up our understanding to the purpose and power of God given favor.

God's deliberate plan for mankind by sending His Son to die for our sins didn't end there. He provided for us an opportunity to grow in His Favor. It would be an absolute waste to know that we all had a wonderful opportunity to have the best of God and walked right by it. Today we are going to stop and take notice of God's continued provision for us as sons and daughters! Favor Here are some of the questions that we will be trying to answer during this series. What is the purpose of favor? What is this force of favor? How does it come? What are the laws and wisdom in which favor is gained and sustained in the lives of believers? How can I determine the measure of favor I walk in? And Jesus grew in wisdom and stature, and in favor with God and men. Luke 2:52

• Favor/ - sha`ah- to look at or to, regard, gaze at or about
• Favor charis- grace; that which affords joy, pleasure, delight, sweetness, charm, loveliness: grace of speech, good will, loving-kindness, favor: of the merciful kindness by which God,

exerting his holy influence upon souls, turns them to Christ, keeps, strengthens, increases them in Christian faith, knowledge, affection, and kindles them to the exercise of the Christian virtues Favor. Jesus' heavenly Sonship did not release Him from His earthly Sonship. In Jesus' developmental years He maintained His fellowship with God, & his fellowship with men.

• He increased – The idea then is strenuous activity rather than passive development. It is to chop forward, to beat forward, to hack on.

• Dean Farrar, "The word used here is derived from pioneers, cutting down trees in the pathway of an advancing army."

• Thayer, "means to lengthen out by hammering as a smith forges metals." Character is what we are; Reputation is what others think of us. Jesus had favor with God and with men. We must understand that as Christ grew in His life, so are we to grow in wisdom, stature, and in favor! You and I need favor in matters with God and man, both in the world and in our spiritual influence on this earth. Marked By God I want us to read and learn about how God chooses to mark you, to use you and to bless you.

1 In the sixth month, God sent the angel Gabriel to Nazareth, a town in Galilee, to a virgin pledged to be married to a man named Joseph, a descendant of David. The virgin's name was Mary. Luke 1:26-27 The angel went to her and said, "Greetings, you who are highly favored! The Lord is with you." Luke 1:28 Mary was greatly troubled at his words and wondered what kind of greeting this might be. Luke 1:29 But the angel said to her, "Do not be afraid, Mary, you have found favor with God. You will be with child and give birth to a son, and you are to give him the name Jesus. Luke 1:30-31 He will be great and will be called the Son of the Most High. The Lord God will give him

the throne of his father David, and he will reign over the house of Jacob forever; his kingdom will never end." Luke 1:32-33 There is no question in this passage that the theme and main focus is on God's purpose of sending to this earth a deliverer in the form of a man, a baby who would grow up and live a perfect life so that His death on the cross could satisfy the price of our sin.

He would, once and for all, satisfy the demands of God's justice by His shed blood. Mohammed couldn't do it, Budda couldn't do it, Chrishna couldn't do it, only God, pre-incarnate, in the form of a man could pay for the sins of the world. That is the message of the gospel. And if you are a Christian today, you know or should already know as a believer in Jesus Christ. What I want to begin today is for us to learn how we can carry the purpose of God for our lives so we can accomplish something significant for Him.

One thing you may be lacking in your life is a strong infusion of the supernatural quality of God that marks you and sets you apart from others so you can carry the purpose of God in your life and bring it to full birth, alive. Highly Favored As you know, God loves us. God loves everyone, but in verse 29, Mary was troubled just like many people are when they begin to discuss the topic of FAVOR, "troubled at His words and wondered what kind of greeting this might be." Notice the words in verse 28, that the angel told her, "You are highly favored! The Lord is with you!"

• Favor charitoō- to make graceful- charming, lovely, agreeable What makes God's love and expression toward Mary so powerful, is because He takes special notice of her. God loves us, I know that for a fact, but there are those occasions in the Bible where God takes special notice of people such as Mary.

• Daniel- Daniel was pleading with God to turn away His wrath upon Jerusalem in Daniel 9, O Lord, listen! O Lord, forgive! O Lord, hear and act! For your sake, O my God, do not delay, because your city and your people bear your Name." Daniel 9:19 And while he was speaking, praying out, confessing his sins and the sins of the people to God, Gabriel appears to him and tells him, As soon as you began to pray, an answer was given, which I have come to tell you, for you are highly esteemed. Therefore, consider the message and understand the vision... Daniel 9:23 • Esteemed H2532 - chemdah- that which is desirable, pleasant and precious Daniel was greatly desired, esteemed!   There was something significant about him that appealed to God and God responded to him with favor! God loves everybody but Daniel has special attention drawn to himself from God.

Mary was someone who had the FAVOR of God. It literally means that she had the peculiar signature of God favor, honor or cherishing placed on her. When He saw her He has a special value placed for her. And when we have the favor of God on us there is a special value that is placed upon us. If you can go there with me, wouldn't it be exciting to be "greatly esteemed" rather than just "esteemed?" Wouldn't you like to find "great favor" more than just "favor" from God? To be greatly beloved is the key to favor! What Happens When The Highly Favor Of God Get's On You? When God highly loves you, there is such a level of influence that falls on you that the very charisma of God Himself rubs off on you which makes other people either like you or cooperate with you weather they like you or not! Every person whose life depends on other relationships to get things done or things completed successfully, athletes, school principles, businessmen, mothers, fathers, needs to understand.

Favor is the special affection of God toward you that releases an influence on you, so that others are inclined to like you or to cooperate with you! How Does Favor Relate To People In The Bible? Mary was given favor and gave birth to Jesus and then Luke gives us a very important scripture that describes Jesus as a child. And Jesus grew in wisdom and stature, and in favor with God and men. Luke 2:52 You can have favor with God but not have very much success in walking in favor with man.

There are a lot of Christians who have not discovered finding favor with man and only believe that they should be concerned with favor with God. Hear me when I say that I am not talking about have a fear of man, I am talking about having a "favor" with man. The truth is, God has more blessing for you than He can get to you. I've met many people who have had the favor of God all over them, with the power of God, the insight of God, and the powerful to believe in great things of God. The Anointing brings favor and favor is in the anointing...but when they are introduced to people, when they are placed in a setting with others, their personality offends, they can't find favor with man.

The favor of God is all over them, but they can't get along with other people. Their anointing brings favor, but the closer you get to them you don't really want to be close to them. On the other side you have those who have favor with men. They have a likable personality, they get along with others and they walk through open doors because of it. But throughout time you don't see the sustaining hand of God in their life. You may see a person who has 3 what is considered success, but not with God.

Their life did not accomplish anything that had the signature of God on it. I think it's imperative that we find out and learn what it is that gives us the favor with God and man. Personally I was taught in opposition to this idea. I was taught that if you had relationship with man then you were cheating with your relationship with God.

I was taught to be suspicious of people and to guard myself from ever being dependent on other relationships. Of course that may sound strange, but I can tell you this, I have favor with God. The anointing brought favor, but I didn't know how to operate within the two worlds.

I was taught that it was compromising to be cooperative with the world and still I was expected to be submitted to it's authorities. I'm telling you that I was confused.

I missed great opportunity in my life for God to bless me and for man to bless me because I did not understand the favor of God and man, and I don't want you to waste another day without it. Here is something that may be a revelation for you, you don't have to walk around unliked, rejected and forgotten and have Jesus. You can allow the whole work of Jesus on the cross to activate in your life. This is not saying you will become a superstar, a hero or popular, but what I am saying is that favor can be a part of your life and you can learn to walk through the doors of those relationship with confidence. Some of you have the favor of man on you and didn't even know it. People like you, they like to ask you questions about their situations, they like being with you and they like giving you opportunity.

A person with favor on them are likable, they are thought of in a positive way. Some of you have never experienced the favor of man over a very long time. You may have constantly felt rejection, being ignored and forgotten. It truly may have something to do with your own personality and attitude, but the truth is, you don't have favor with man. You are not on anyone's radar when they are looking for someone to hire, someone to confide in or someone to have a relationship with. This is not to be cruel, this is a fact, you don't have the favor of man and that needs to change in your life! The true men and women in the Bible who walked in favor stirred up envy and jealousy in others around them, but they didn't stir up unjustified opposition because there was a grace on them.

Jesus walked in favor with both God and man. In John 7:25-47, Jesus was teaching in the temple courts and the people crowded around and became divided. Some said he was a prophet, to others He was the Christ, still others wanted to arrest Him, but no one laid a hand on Him.

The temple priest sent their guards to arrest Him. When the guards came back without Jesus the chief priest and the Pharisees asked why they hadn't arrested Him, the guards answered, "No one has ever talked like this before!" Jesus found favor.

Yes He was a gifted and anointed speaker, but something deeper leaped on the people. Jesus found favor in the eyes of the community that day...even those who wanted to do Him hard could not act on it. Many of you have experienced favor in the most unusual situations. Favor will come when you don't expect it, as a matter of fact it can over take you causing other people to cooperate with you, causing them the talk to you, to be nice to you, to open doors of opportunity for you.

Esther Vashti was the queen of King Xerxes. She refused to come before him when he asked for her and so the King looked for another queen. In Esther 2:15, the Bible says that a search went out to find another queen.

When the turn came for Esther (the girl Mordecai had adopted, the daughter of his uncle Abihail) to go to the king, she asked for nothing other than what Hegai, the king's eunuch who was in charge of the harem, suggested. And Esther won the favor of everyone who saw her. Esther 2:15 Now the king was attracted to Esther more than to any of the other women, and she won his favor and approval more than any of the other virgins.

So he set a royal crown on her head and made her queen instead of Vashti. Esther 2:17 The Favor of God is what inclines people's attention toward you. It really doesn't matter what you look like or what your education is or what your background is when you have the God's Spirit of favor on you.. Daniel Now God had caused the official to show favor and sympathy to Daniel... Daniel 1:9 Now here is an important point to make in relationship to Esther. Notice that both Daniel and Esther are both in a foreign country, he was in the minority, a despised people, a conquered people. In both Daniel and Esther we have evidence where God will take those who are down trodden, and those in a disadvantaged position and will cause them to be promoted. He was going to be called in front of the King just like Esther.

At this time Daniel was from the age of 14-18, uprooted from his family, taken captive with the rest of Israel by the Babylonian empire. But the favor of God was upon Daniel and he had favor with man too! Verse 9 says that God caused the official, the KJV calls him the Prince of the Kings eunuchs.

And not only does Daniel have this individuals attention, but the Bible says that the official showed Daniel favor and sympathy.

It's a much stronger word than that. The original says that the official had tender love, he had mercy, compassion and pity on Daniel. The favor of God was on Daniel and the result is Daniel was going to become the vice-president of the nation, succeeding four different empires. How could this happen? God brought Daniel into favor and tender love. God provided a Spirit of inclination to give Daniel favor to the success of the kingdom.

What we want to learn throughout this series is how to walk in favor with God and Man! When you have the favor of man you can do extraordinary things with your life for God's glory. I believe that you and I as the body of Jesus Christ needs a solid dose of the favor of God! I believe that we should be the influencers rather than the cleaner-uppers. We should not be dealing with everyone jumping off the cliffs of sin, we should be at the top of our nation helping millions of people avoid the destructive spiral of a life without God! We should not be in the back seat but next to the driver.

We have taken a seat too far from the point of the spear. We have more faith in our children failing, our economy failing, our relationships failing that God having any influence at all. We have got to reposition ourselves and allow God to place a spirit of favor on our lives so He can have the glory of winning. Redeemed If you are a believer and you have made a decision to not only receive Christ, but to follow Christ, that means that you have exchanged your desires and ways to come into align with His desires and ways, then when God sees you, He sees you in harmony with His heart. The Bible calls it Righteousness, or walking upright. It's not perfection, but it is pure.

In your past, it doesn't matter how horrible or weak or fearful you were. When you received Jesus Christ you received the full work of Jesus Christ. Jesus didn't give you a little portion of Himself, He gave you all of Himself. God's remedy for your past was to kill you. That's what the cross is, Jesus Christ taking your place. When Jesus died for you He died as you and in Christ, you are dead and He is alive. When you are reminded of something in your past you need to remind yourself that you are thinking of a person who is no longer alive. Satan attempts to bring a dead man to life by reading his biography.

You should say in your heart and mind, I'm so glad that person no longer lives! Anything in your past prior to the saving grace of Jesus Christ is a biography of another person. You are free! You are redeemed! When you receive this fully you will no longer be self-conscience, or awkward around people, fumbling your words and actions, you won't be touchy, resentful, over sensitive, hyper, easily irritated or addicted, you are free! And here's why, YOU ARE DEAD! Those who have come to the fulness of God's great love in them allow Him to do a work in them that you can't read enough books for, get enough counseling for, go to enough seminars for and be schooled enough for. When you can fully reckon yourself dead and that you are alive in Christ and that the circumstances surrounding you do not dictate who you are because of the blood of Jesus Christ, you will find favor! When you have ceased from trying to perfect your life to get the approval of God.

Have stopped striving to get His attention and you fall fully on the Grace of God, and you receive the FULL WORK OF JESUS CHRIST. Then the Holy Spirit can lead you into the freedom that you so badly want and whom the Son sets free is free indeed! God cannot and will not give you more, because what Jesus Christ has provided on the cross was enough to satisfy God almighty and defeat Satan totally.

This is one great deal! But if you cannot grab ahold of the full work of Christ then you will continue to labor, attempting to get the favor of God and man. You will labor your hardest for Christ and will not be yoked with Him. Joseph Because the patriarchs were jealous of Joseph, they sold him as a slave into Egypt. But God was with him and rescued him from all his troubles. He gave Joseph wisdom and enabled him to gain the goodwill of Pharaoh king of Egypt; so he made him ruler over Egypt and all his palace. Acts 7:9-10 God was with Joseph and gave him wisdom and favor with the king of Egypt to become a ruler. Here is something powerful to think about. Not only does God's favor give Joseph promotion but also supernatural ability of wisdom with the promotion. God Enables You When He Relabels You!

1. Favor Produces Envy The favor of God also gave Joseph wisdom to live up to the level of his favor! Why was Joseph in prison in the first place? It was because of the envy of others. Do you really want the favor of God on your life? The other side of having an anointing of the favor of God is to be in a high degree of spiritual warfare. And when you are blessed with the favor of God there is something that you have to deal with, people who see and discern favor on you but don't see favor on themselves will envy what it is that you have and will try to find something wrong with what you have. This is the very reason why Daniel ended up in the Lion's den.

He was in the lion's den because all the other officials and leaders began to resent the unique characteristic quality that made people like him and were inclined to cooperate with him. So, people who don't have favor will be jealous of you and will attempt to sabotage your favor. They will try to ruin your character, attack everything about you. They hate your success and will look at ever opportunity to discredit you. When we look at Joseph, we also can look at Jesus. When Pilate was deliberating what to do with Jesus, the Bible says that Pilate perceived, For he knew it was out of envy that they had handed Jesus over to him. Matthew 27:18 Favor has a price and you must learn to walk in the boldness of the Lord because when favor is on your life there will be those who do not like it and will come against you.

2. Favor Produces Temptation Not everyone is opposed to the favor that can come upon you. Satan is very desirous of that favor on you. He once lived in the favor of God and he wants so badly to have that back. He is especially envious and jealous of it. In Joseph's story, he was the leader of Potiphar's house. He had so much favor with his boss that Potiphar's wife was attracted to him. That favor put him in a position that could have easily caused him to sacrifice his integrity.

What happens when you have too much favor? You have to make sure you are rooted and grounded in the Word of God and into Jesus' character or you will find yourself in a compromising position...one you didn't think you were a part of but you got blamed for. What Does Favor Do? King Saul sends for David, and when David stood before King Saul, verse 21, he loved him greatly! Favor is the inclination to like. There was an immediate connection between them. Then Saul sent to Jesse, saying, "Please let David stand before me, for he has found favor in my sight." I Samuel 16:22 (NKJV) Where Does This Power Come From? What would happen if you had the full force of favor operating on you? It would be so amazing that when you were with people and suddenly their heart would be the same heart God has toward you. Favor is people experiencing God's affection toward you. How do I know this? Because in about two chapters later, Saul is attempting to kill David. Saul loses his affection toward him.

Can you imagine that God could trust you with this on you and you were a salesman? You could persuade people to buy or to make certain decisions or persuade them toward God! While they are in the presence of you, the presence of favor comes on them. Favor allows you to multiply your natural talent and at times it can go beyond talent all together. It was Paul, in Acts 17 who persuaded some of the Jews to join them, as did a large number of God-fearing Greeks and not a few prominent women. But the Jews were jealous; so they rounded up some bad characters from the marketplace, formed a mob and started a riot in the city...These men who have caused trouble all over the world have now come here... Acts 17:5a, 6b It was Paul's influence to persuade others to follow Christ that turned the world upside down! There is an anointing that lifts you above your game. It places you at a whole other level.

You would think that you wouldn't have favor until you have some real good enemies! How Did Favor Get Transmitted To David? The transaction took place when Samuel was going through the sons of the house of Jesse. As he was looking for who he was supposed to anoint, Samuel had to ask Jesse if all the boys were there, Jesse said there was still one out in the field. See, there was one out in the fields watching the sheep. One that didn't really make the cut in our eyes. One that wasn't worth your time. We've got that one, but are you sure? See, David was the joke. David was the one that didn't fit in. David spent a lot of time alone and none of his brothers thought anything about him. Samuel could tell that the favor of God was not on any of those boys like he had felt in his heart.

There was an awareness that he had for the right person. It was more than a gut feeling, it was an anointing! So he sent and had him brought in. He was ruddy, with a fine appearance and handsome features. Then the Lord said, "Rise and anoint him; he is the one." I Samuel 16:12 So Samuel took the horn of oil and anointed him in the presence of his brothers, and from that day on the Spirit of the Lord came upon David in power... I Samuel 16:13 The anointing is released which releases the Holy Spirits power. The Lord's anointing puts the favor of God on you. The moment that the anointing came on David, favor fell on David. God favored David, why, because David had something in himself that attracted God. What was it? But the Lord said to Samuel, "Do not consider his appearance or his height, for I have rejected him. The Lord does not look at the things man looks at. Man looks at the outward appearance, but the Lord looks at the heart." I Samuel 16:7 God puts His favor on those who's heart are set in motion toward Him. There is a lot of people whose heart is in pursuit toward God.

Two Affects of Favor:
1. God's attraction to you.
2. The power of influence through you.

Whenever the spirit from God came upon Saul, David would take his harp and play. Then relief would come to Saul; he would feel better, and the evil spirit would leave him. I Samuel 16:23 When you are walking in the anointing of God, the favor of God, it empowers you to not only have God's favor and man's favor, but it gives you favor over the powers of darkness. When you are walking in your anointing, the favor of God in you can bind the power of Satan in others! When you are walking in the Spirit of favor it produces a perimeter of divine influence that brings everything under the authority of the agenda that God is given you to accomplish.

When favor is on your life, there are those who are in the radius of your destiny, a divine perimeter is established so that your influence takes authority over the devils agenda and in that arena, your agenda begins to emerge supreme! Here is the secret of Daniel, the secret of Easter, of David, Joseph and even Mary. They were all connected to Kingdom Building. Now see if this scripture looks a little different in light of what I just said, But seek first his kingdom and his righteousness, and all these things will be given to you as well. Matthew 6:33 God is always and will always be involved in kingdoms.

He raises and lowers a kingdom. The closer and committed you are to the purpose and principles of God's kingdom, the more He can have favor on you. Your influence in expanding the kingdom expands with the favor you obtain. But can you weather the storms of jealousy and envy and can you overcome the temptations that come with that success? God doesn't give favor for people just to make more money and to have more friends. He gives them favor for the same reason that He would give Esther, Joseph and Daniel favor, so they could influence a kingdom. He put a spirit of favor on David because he was going to take over a kingdom. And God is giving you favor to take over kingdoms and influence them for Him and His glory.

Realms of Favors

"And whatever you do, do it with all your heart as for the Lord and not man, knowing that the Lord will reward you." Colossians 3:23,24

And rescued him from all his troubles. He granted Joseph favor and wisdom in the sight of Pharaoh king of Egypt, who appointed him ruler over Egypt and all his household. Acts 7:10

And the LORD was with Joseph, and he became a successful man, serving in the household of his Egyptian master. Genesis 39:2

1. Law of Difference – Gen 1:27; Heb 2:6-7; Ps 8:5
a. It is your difference that is the greatest asset you have
b. You do not need to try to be like someone else
c. You do not need someone just like you
d. You do not marry someone just like you

2. Law of Protecting your mind – Ps 101:3-4; Rom 12:9
a. Fill your mind with good stuff
b. Avoid the bad stuff

3. Law of Recognition – Rom 12:6-17
a. Recognize the opportunities
b. Recognize the gifts in others
c. Recognize your gifts

4. Law of Two – Ecc 4:9-12; Deut 32:30; Matt 18:20;
a. It takes two for almost anything

b. It takes two to multiply (most of the time)

c. One can put 1,000 to flight but two can put 10,000

d. Two are better than one

e. Where two or more are gathered

f. The two shall become one

5. Law of Place – Gen 12:1-3

a. Where you are is as important as what you are

b. Where you are is as important as who you are

c.
God has directed you to where you are and God can do anything "where you are"

d. When you are where you belong, God can use you and no one can hurt you

e. Provisions are the confirmation you are where you are supposed to be

6. Law of Honor – Est 6:6-10

a.
Your future is determined by who you have chosen to honor

b. Honor those who are deserving of honor

c.
Be careful who you dishonor, it may cause you to fail in life

d. Who you honor may determine your success in life

7. Law of the Seed – Gal 6:7-8

a. You reap what you sow

b. You reap later than you sow

c. You reap more than you sow

A Gift called Favor

Now that we've dealt with your self-esteem and you now realize how special you are to God, let's define favor. Exactly what is favor? Favor is something granted out of good will rather than for justice or payment. In other words, it is a gift from God. You didn't earn it. You can't buy it. You can't be so good that finally God will say, "You've been so good, you've earned favor." It is also defined as a gift bestowed as a token of regard, love or friendliness (or friendship) and preferential treatment. It's what Jesus did at Calvary that earned you the favor of God.

We use this word "favor" in our every day language. Sometimes you ask someone, "Would you do a favor for me?" What are you saying? "Just how strong is our relationship? Is God our relationship so strong that you would do this for me without question?" That's a favor. Then we start reading about favor from the Bible and get into a church that has some stained glass windows and some pews, and we think "favor" has a "religious" meaning, but it's the same thing. In fact, God wants you to ask Him for favors.

Not too long ago, a friend of mine who is a Christian businessman, came to me after a service I was ministering in and said, "Brother Jerry, I really need for you to pray over my business. This thing is falling apart. If God doesn't give us supernatural intervention, we're going to lose it all." He said, "I know God gave me this business and God has blessed me through this business. It is just an all out attack of the Devil."

I've known this man a long time and when he said that, I could sense how overwhelmed he was by this. The compassion of the Lord Jesus began to rise up in me and I took his hand and

80

started praying for him but I heard something come out of me that I don't think I had ever prayed before. I said "Lord Jesus, as a favor to me, intervene in my friend's behalf."

I don't ever remember a time where I had prayed like that. Usually I'd say, "Father, in the Name of Jesus..." and I'd quote the Word, but I didn't that time. That man called me three days later and said," "God gave us a supernatural breakthrough!" He said, I don't know what you said, but God came through, hallelujah!"

So, I asked the Lord, "How come You did that so fast?"
He said, "Because you asked Me for a favor."
I said, "Glory to God, do I carry that much weight with You?"
He said, "You do." He said, "You don't realize it but you have that kind of favor." Then He said, "Wouldn't you do the same thing for Me if I came to you and said, 'Jerry I need a favor?'" Of course I would!

Religion wants it to be so hard to get the ear of God. Religion wants you to think you've got to be so good, and have all this merit, but the Bible says, "He's full of compassion." I believe many sinners stay sinners because they've had the wrong image of God portrayed to them. Most sinners don't know the goodness of God. All they know about God is what they've heard from most Christians. "Thou shalt not... If thou do, thou shalt die...."

They hear that God is just looking for an opportunity to knock their brains out. That's what I thought before I began serving the Lord. That's the image that Christians gave me. I thought, "Dear God, I know the Devil is trying to kill me, and now I'm going to serve God and He's going to try to kill me too. I haven't got a chance."

But then I got into the Word of God and found out that I'd been lied to. I found out that God is gracious. God is full of compassion. God is merciful. He's plenteous in mercy and not only that, the nature of God is to show favors.

I found out that the more of the nature of God that is imparted into me as a result of the Word and as a result of fellowship with Him, the more I am disposed to show favors to others. You become like God. You become full of mercy. You become compassionate. You become one that people can ask for favors.

The Lord is merciful, gracious, slow to anger and plenteous in mercy.
Psalm 103:8

Did you hear that? You're not making God mad all the time. Even when you foul up, God's not saying, "Where's Michael— my war angel... Kill them." No. He's slow to anger. He's a good God.

In the Hebrew many times the words "mercy" and "compassion" are interchangeable, and, in some cases, defined as "disposed to show favors." In other words, the very nature of God is disposed to show favor. God can't help Himself, He is so good, He's disposed to show favors.
Psalm 5:12 says,

For thou, Lord, wilt bless the righteous; with favor wilt thou compass him as with a shield.
The Amplified Bible says,
. . . as with a shield You will surround him with good will (pleasure and favor).

"Pleasure" is an area that religion doesn't teach us either. God does not mind you having pleasure. Religion doesn't want you to have any fun! I'm glad I never became religious. I love God with all my heart. I'm sold out and deeply committed to God but I'm not religious. Even before I became a Christian—

I've always had somewhat of a joyful nature. I was always the class clown. I was always making folks laugh. It wasn't something I tried to do. It was just my nature.

But when I got around people who tried to get me to become a Christian, I thought, Dear God, if I ever become a Christian, I'll never laugh again. Humor seemed to have no place in religion. I thought, I'll have to change my whole personality if I get saved. I'll have to take on this wrinkled, prune face look...never laugh...never have any joy...just sit in the corner reading the Bible all day—join a convent or become a monk.

Then I found out that God has a sense of humor. He wanted to change me from death unto life, but He wanted to use my personality. And He wants to use your personality too! God gave you your personality. So notice, He says, as with as shield You will surround him with good will (pleasure and favor) (Psalm 5:12). God will surround you with pleasure. Your Christianity ought to be fun. It ought to be so much fun that sinners become envious.

Now don't think, "Brother Jerry just never has any problems." I have problems just like you. I have adversity just like you. I have opposition just like you. I have to stand on the Word of God constantly, just like you. But the beautiful part is, I know that I have the favor of God and somehow, some way before this thing is all said and done, and before the dust settles, I'll win. I have the favor of God, hallelujah. He's never failed me. Never!

Do you realize what the favor of God will do in your life? It will open doors that men say are impossible to open. It will change rules, regulations, policies and even bring down governments, if necessary, to get you through a door God wants you through. The favor of God will turn every adversity in your life into a victory, praise God.

Grace [or favor] be with all them that love our Lord Jesus Christ in sincerity.
Ephesians 6:24

Another word for "grace" is unmerited favor. So, when you see the word "grace" you could interchange it with the word "favor." The Apostle Paul says, "For everyone who walks with God and is sincere about that walk, favor be unto them."

Don't get mad at others if doors open for them that don't open to you. You can have preferential treatment too. Don't get mad when others are blessed. You can be just as blessed. Don't

get mad because you hear testimonies of wonderful things happening in others lives. You are highly favored of the Lord, but you need to learn how to walk in divine favor.

The Bible says that God is no respecter of persons. That means that the same preferential treatment they get, you can have too.

Obviously, if you don't have a revelation of it, then you can't walk in it. A lack of knowledge will cause you to live way below your privileges. But once you have a revelation of how special you are to God, then you will be able to walk in favor.

Instead of having low self-esteem, no confidence and just taking everything the Devil dishes out, we ought to be walking around with our heads held high knowing full well that we have preferential treatment with Almighty God! You and I are honored by God.

Walking in Favor

Proverbs 14:9 says,
Fools make a mock at sin: hut among the righteous there is favour.
In Genesis 12:1, God is speaking to Abraham and says,

Now the Lord had said unto Abram, Get thee out of thy country, and from thy kindred, and from thy father's house, unto a land that I will shew thee; And I will make of thee a great nation, and I will bless thee, and make thy name great; and thou shalt be a blessing.

The Amplified Bible says verse 2 this way:
And I will make you a great nation and I will bless you with an abundant increase of favors.

Notice the purpose of this covenant. God says that His intent for establishing covenant with Abraham was to give God an avenue by which He could bring blessings into Abram's life, and it would give God a channel to increase favor in the man's life. He said, I will bless you with an abundant increase of favors. In other words, God is saying, "I'd like to do favors for you, and I'd like to do them in abundance."

You may be thinking, "That's what He said to Abram, not me." Yes, but this also applied to the seed of Abram (or Abraham). In Galatians 3:29 it says, And if ye be Christ's, then are ye Abraham's seed, and heirs according to the promise. So you are entitled! Through this covenant, God has established a

WALKING IN DIVINE FAVOR channel by which you are entitled to walk in the favor of God.

All you have to do is study Abraham's life and you see favor. Genesis 24:1 says,
And Abraham was old, and well stricken in age: and the Lord had blessed Abraham in all things.
God had favored him in all things. The favor of God in Abraham's life caused his wife's barren womb to conceive. The favor of God will even change medical reports. The favor of God will change what men say is impossible.

DECLARE FAVOR!
When God began ministering to me about His favor, I realized that I had let that revelation slip. The Lord said to me, "Son, you're not believing Me for favor like you used to. You could be walking in a whole lot more favor than what you're walking in if you'd believe Me for it. Consciously ask Me for favors." So I started.

I made up my mind, if I'm entitled to more favor, then I'm going to walk in it. I'm not just going to say, "Amen, hallelujah, praise God." No, I'm going to commit to it and actually walk in it. I do not let a day go by without confessing "I walk in divine favor. The favor of God goes before me today, changing rules, regulations and policies."

I not only confess it for me but I confess it for my children. I confess that this family walks in the favor of God And we do. Some of it is happening so instantly that it is overwhelming!
I challenge you to study favor and begin to confess the favor of God in your life. Be consistent with it. Don't just try it for 3 or 4 days and quit if you don't see any results. Be diligent about it. Revelation is going to come to you where the favor of God is

concerned, and it is going to lift your self-esteem and your confidence. It's going to make you feel like you are somebody in the sight of God. Things that you've been struggling with for a long time are going to come to pass simply because you realize that you have favor with God.

You need to start declaring the favor of God. Confess the favor of God. Get up in the morning and say, "This is another day that the Lord has made, I will rejoice and be glad therein. The favor of God goes before me and surrounds me. You'll be amazed at doors that will start opening for you. Declare the favor of God! Decree the favor of God goes before you! And

Increate thy Favor

Luke 2:52 states, And Jesus increased in wisdom and stature and in favour with God and man. From this verse, we see that we can increase in the favor of God. Let's see how this takes place in our lives.

1. CONSIDER YOUR WAYS

I intreated thy favour with my whole heart: be merciful unto me according to thy word. I thought on my ways, and turned my feet unto thy testimonies.
Psalm 119:58,59

The Psalmist is asking for more favor. Notice in verse 59, it reveals to us what he did to increase in favor. He said, I thought on my ways.... Obviously, if you are going to ask for favor to be increased, then your lifestyle must be pleasing to God.

Your lifestyle has everything to do with favor increasing in your life. Remember what God said in Haggai 1:5-7.
Now therefore thus says the Lord of hosts; Consider your ways [and set your mind on what has come to you]. You have sown much, but you have reaped little; you eat, but you do not have enough; you drink, but you do not have your fill; you clothe yourselves, but no one is warm; and he who earns wages has earned them to put them in a bag with holes in it. Thus says the Lord of Hosts: Consider your ways...
(The Amplified Bible)

Consider your ways. Notice it didn't say, "Consider God's ways." There's nothing wrong with God's ways. The Amplified

Version says, Consider your ways, your previous and present conduct. (v.7) I did a study on this verse and found that "ways" could be defined as course of action, methods and manners,
conduct and behavior. In other words, your course of action, your methods and manners, your conduct and your behavior have everything to do with whether or not you increase in the favor of God.

So if you want to increase in God's favor, then take an inventory of your ways. If you find things in your life that you know are not pleasing to God, then correct them. Take authority over them, and get them out of your life so that you can begin to walk in a greater level of God's favor.

2. CONTINUALLY SEEK GOD

Hear instruction, and be wise, and refuse it not. Blessed is the man that heareth me, watching daily at my gates, wailing at the posts of my doors. For whoso findeth me findeth life, and shall obtain favour of the Lord.
Proverbs 8:33-35

Findeth me... is a key to increasing in God's favor. Continually seek Him and keep your ears open to His voice and listen to His instructions for your life. Learn to be sensitive so you can hear His voice clearly. How do you find Him? By spending quality time with Him. Spend time reading His Word
and praying in the Spirit so that you can get to know Him more intimately. The more intimate your fellowship with Him becomes, the more of His favor you'll experience.

3. BE OBEDIENT

Be obedient to God's instructions. Obviously, the more obedient you are to God, the more capability you have of increasing in His favor. People who are disobedient don't walk in favor. When you hear God's instructions, don't hesitate—be quick to obey. The person who will do that will not only find life, but he'll walk in a greater level of the favor of the Lord.

4. HUNGER FOR TRUTH

My son, forget not my law; but let thine heart keep my commandments: For length of days, and long life, and peace, shall they add to thee. Let not mercy and truth forsake thee: bind them about thy neck; write them upon the table of thine heart: So shalt thou find favour and good understanding in the sight of God and man.

Proverbs 3:1-4 Create a hunger for truth. Seek it with all of your heart. When God sees how much you love truth, then favor will increase in your life. God delights in those who love truth. Remember, Jesus said that those who continue in His Word shall know the truth and the truth shall make them free.

5. STRIVE FOR EXCELLENCE

He that diligently seeketh good procureth favour: but he that seeketh mischief, it shall come unto him.
Proverbs 11:27

What does He mean by this? In other words, develop a lifestyle of seeking out that which is good and pleasing to God. Don't always look for the shortcuts in life. Look for the things that put a demand on your life to become the best you can possibly be. Look for ways to be a blessing to others. When you are favorable toward others then more favor comes to you.

6. DON'T EVER LOSE YOUR ZEAL FOR THE WORD

Whoso despiseth the word shall he destroyed: but he that feareth the commandment shall be rewarded. The law of the wise is a fountain of life, to depart from the snares of death. Good understanding giveth favour.
Proverbs 13:13,14

Notice he says, Whoso despiseth the Word... I've seen this happen to many Christians: "I'm so tired of studying the Word! I'm so tired of having to be in the Word all the time." The Word has become irksome to them. They've lost their zeal for the Word. They used to be zealous. They bought all the Christian books. They bought all the most inspirational tapes. They went to all the seminars. They couldn't get enough of the Word. But then, you don't see them quite as frequently. You notice they don't talk the Word like they used to.

Do you know anyone like this? They've lost their desire for the Word. According to this scripture, when you lose your zeal for the Word, you literally cut yourself off from increased favor. Never lose your zeal for the Word. Never lose your hunger for revelation knowledge and always desire understanding! Good understanding giveth favor. The more you understand God's ways, the more you're going to walk in His favor.

Favor in Your Time

And he said, Do it the second time. And they did it the second time. And he said, Do it the third time. And they did it the third time. 1 Kings 18:34

Next, he arranged the wood, cut up the bull, placed it on the wood, 1 Kings 18:33
So the water ran down around the altar and even filled the trench. 1 Kings 18:35 4

Have you ever been overwhelmed by anything? Have you ever had a problem that consumed your mind 24 hours a day and there seemed to be no solution to it? In Psalm 102, we read about a man who is completely overwhelmed by his situation, he needs an answer from God, and he needs it immediately. See if you can relate.

Here my prayer O Lord and let my cry come unto thee. Hide not thy face from me in the day when I am in trouble; incline thine ear unto me: in the day when I call answer me speedily (vv. 1,2).

He's getting right to the point. "God, I need an answer, and I need it real fast." He goes on to say in verses 3 to 13,
For my days are consumed like smoke and my bones are burned as a hearth. My heart is smitten, and withered like grass: so that I forget to eat my bread. By reason of the voice of my groaning my bones cleave to my skin. I am like a pelican of the wilderness: I am like an owl in the desert.

I watch, and am a sparrow alone upon the house top. Mine enemies reproach me all the day; and they that are mad against me are sworn against me. For I have eaten ashes like bread, and mingled my drink with weeping, Because of thine indignation and thy wrath: for thou hast lifted me up, and cast me down. My days are like a shadow that declineth: and I am withered like grass. But thou, 0 Lord, shalt endure, for ever; and thy remembrance unto all generations. Thou shall arise, and have, mercy upon Zion: for the time to favor her, yea, the set time, is come.

Notice that even though this man is overwhelmed by his adversity, he still recognizes that he is entitled to the favor of God. When many of us are faced with overwhelming situations, it's easy to become problem-minded rather than solution-minded. We tend to forget our covenant during a trial. Sometimes the problem can be so overwhelming that it's all you can think about. But notice in the midst of all of this, the Psalmist remembers that he is entitled to God's favor. The reason he knows he is entitled to it is because he's a covenant man.

Notice he says, Thou shall arise and have mercy upon Zion for the time to favor her, yea the set time is come.

Once he begins to get his mind off the problem and starts thinking about the favor of God, he begins to speak more positively. He begins to talk about what God will do when He arises and what the favor of God will do when it comes on the scene. You need to realize that no matter what you are going through and no matter how severe it is, you are entitled to the favor of God, but you need to learn to expect that favor.

The Amplified says it this way,

93

... the moment designated has come... There is a moment designated for the favor of God to come.

Every time you have been under pressure, and your situation looked impossible, the Devil said, "There is no way," but God always seemed to find a way. Isn't that right!" Well, that was a manifestation of the favor of God. When you expect it to come, it will cause you to remain positive and change your perspective about your outcome.

A TESTIMONY

What once was an overwhelming test can be turned into a testimony. The Devil hopes you will forget that God's favor is available. He'd like for you to stay overwhelmed. Sometimes you just need to rehearse in your mind all the victories that you've had with God. Just think about them. This is a great weapon against the adversary, particularly when he is endeavoring to overwhelm you with a problem. Say to yourself, "Hey wait a minute, I've been through adversity before. I've faced impossible situations before. Let me recall what God did the last time!"

When you start recalling how God delivered you, how God healed you and how God made a way, it causes your faith to be energized. Obviously, Satan doesn't want your faith to be energized because he knows your faith will overcome his attacks.

CHANGE ATTITUDE

Perspective is very important. When David was confronted with Goliath, he had a totally different perspective than his brothers did. They saw a man too big to kill, but David saw a man too big to miss. Same giant, same problem, but a different perspective.

In the verses which we previously read, I believe the Psalmist starts out talking out about how overwhelmed he is by his problems. But in a few moments, He begins to think about the mercy of God, the love of God, the favor of God and his position with God, and suddenly, his attitude changes.

He says, "The set time has come for Your favour to be manifested in my life." He expects it and God does it. God wants to pour out His favor. He wants to manifest His favor in your life, but it will not come until you have a change of attitude. Don't give in to the Devil, but expect the favor of God to show up in your life and it will every time.

THE BEST

Quit saying, "Nothing good ever happens to me." You are highly honored and favored of God. That's the reason Paul calls you the elect of God. One definition of the word "elect" is "hand picked" You are hand picked by God. God accepted what Jesus did at Calvary; therefore, He accepted those for whom Jesus died and has made us righteousness. You are in right standing with God; therefore, expect to walk in His favor.

I walk in humility, but at the same time, I expect to be favored. I expect doors to be opened for me that might not open for someone else. I expect to be blessed coming in and blessed going out. I expect to be blessed in the city and blessed in the field. Do you understand what I'm saying? Not because of what I've done but because of what Jesus has done.

You are an ambassador for Christ. Stop and think about it.

Ambassadors of nations are highly favored and get preferential treatment. When they represent their nation, they get preferential treatment. They ride around in big cars with flags on the fenders, and they have escorts leading them to the embassy. Why? They are ambassadors. We think of being an ambassador for Christ as some kind of second rate thing, but we represent the Kingdom of Almighty God. We're not talking about representing Nigeria or the United States or Canada. We're talking about representing a Kingdom that cannot be shaken, praise God. We're representing the Kingdom of the Most High God.

THE TOP

The Bible reveals to us that when the favor of God is surrounding you like a shield then every adversity is turned into victory. We have an example in Genesis 39 of a man named Joseph who experienced adversity all around him. But, because the favor of God was on him and surrounded him, God turned every adversity into a victory.

Remember the story of how his brothers had deceived him and he was brought into captivity?
And the Lord was with Joseph, and he was a prosperous man; and he was in the house of his master the Egyptian. And his master saw that the Lord was with him, and that the Lord made all that he did to prosper in his hand.

Prosper Through Favor

Genesis 39:2,3
What a testimony! Even the Egyptians recognized that God's hand was upon him and that God made everything he did to prosper, Why was the man prospering? Because he was favored. Notice this happened even when he was in captivity. It didn't make any difference where Joseph was, he came out on top.

And Joseph found grace in his sight, and he served him: and he made him overseer over his house, and all that he had he put into his hand.

Genesis 39:4
The favor of God was on Joseph to the point that even his master, Potiphar, saw that this man was highly favored of God and he put him in charge of everything.

And it came to pass from the time that he had made him overseer in his house, and over all that he had, that the Lord blessed the Egyptian's house for Joseph's sake; and the blessing of the Lord was upon all that he had in the house, and in the field. And he left all that he had in Joseph's hand; and he knew not ought he had, save the bread which he did eat. And Joseph was a godly person, and well favoured.

Genesis 39:5,6
Here is a man who is supposed to be a slave and his master has turned everything over to him. He's so confident in Joseph's integrity and the favour of God that is on him that he just turns it

all over to him and gives him total trust and confidence. Why? The favor of God was on Joseph.

Then, Potiphar's wife tries to seduce Joseph, and he won't have anything to do with her. Time and time again, she tries to seduce him, but his integrity will not allow him to compromise. Don't you wish there were more men and women like this today?

Because Joseph refuses her, she plots against him. When he constantly refuses her seduction, one day she grabs him as he's in her quarters and tries to seduce him. Still he will not yield. He will not compromise. He begins to run out, but she grabs his coat and hangs onto it. When his master returns, she lies about it and says that Joseph seduced her showing him the coat for proof. Did you notice in this, Joseph never defended himself! He never said, "Your wife is lying." He didn't have to defend himself? He knew the favor of God was on him and that the favor of God would vindicate him. Of course the master believes his wife and Joseph ends up being thrown into prison, but that's not the end of the story.

But the Lord was with Joseph, and shewed him mercy, and gave him favour in the sight the keeper of the prison. And the keeper of the prison committed to Joseph's hand all the prisoners that were in the prison; and whatsoever they did there, he was the doer of it.

Genesis 39:21,22

He was thrown in prison, and then became the warden. That's favor! You cannot stop this man from being victorious. God's favor causes him to rise to the top every time. That's what the favor of God will do.

Verse 23 says:

The keeper of the prison looked not to anything that was under his hand; because the Lord was with him, and that which he did, the Lord made it to prosper.

He just keeps being promoted! Notice what it says after Joseph interpreted Pharoah's dream.

And Pharaoh said unto Joseph, For as much as God hath shewed thee all this, there is none so discreet and wise as thou art;
And Pharaoh took off his ring from his hand, and put it upon Joseph's hand, and arrayed him in vestures of fine linen, and put a gold chain about his neck.

Genesis 41:39,42
This man was a slave, a prisoner, and a captive. His brothers deceived him, he was sold into slavery, and Pharoah winds up setting the entire land of Egypt under Joseph's oversight!

Verse 46 says:

And Joseph was thirty years old when he stood before Pharaoh king of Egypt.

This all happened to a young man because the favor of God was on him. That's what the favor of God will do. That's the reason you and I need to declare His favor. Even when the Devil tries to take us to the lowest pit, we will always rise to the top because of the favor of God.

Favor in Victories

When you walk in favor, it will bring victories in your life that you cannot acquire in your own strength and in your own might.

Psalm 44:1-3 says,

We have heard with our ears, 0 God, our fathers have told us, what work thou didst in their days, in the times of old. How thou didst drive out the heathen with thy hand, and plantedst them; how thou didst afflict the people, and cast them out. For they got not the land in possession by their own sword, neither did their own arm save them: but thy right hand, and thine arm, and the light of thy countenance, because thou hadst a favor unto them.

When they couldn't take the land by their own might, by their own strength, by their own intelligence or ability, God's favor came on them, and they were able to possess the land God had promised them.

You can either war in your own might, or you can rest in the favor of God. And when the favor of God goes before you, it will enable you to take possession of what is rightfully yours. The favor of God will help you win battles that you could never win in your own strength.

Favor produces supernatural increase and promotion

Genesis 39:21

1. Favor produces restoration of everything that the enemy has stolen from you.

Exodus 3:21

2. Favor produces honor in the midst of your adversaries.

Exodus 11:3

3. Favor produces increased assets, especially in the area of real estate.

Deuteronomy 33:23

4. Favor produces great victories in the midst of great impossibilities.

Joshua 11:20

5. Favor produces recognition, even when you seem the least likely to receive it.

I Samuel 16:22

6. Favor produces prominence and preferential treatment.

Esther 2:17

7. Favor produces petitions granted even by ungodly civil authorities.

Esther 5:8

8. Favor causes policies, rules, regulations and laws to be changed and reversed to your advantage. Esther 8:5

9. Favor produces battles won which you won't even fight because God will fight them for you. Psalm 44:3

Favor Creates Confidence

When the favor of God is upon you and goes before you, then you can walk with your head up high. You can walk with a sense of confidence and security knowing full well that God is on your side.

Psalm 89:17 says,

For thou art the glory of their strength: and in thy favour our horn shall he exalted.

For you are the glory of their strength [their proud adornment], and by, Your favor our horn is exalted and we walk with up lifted faces!

The people of God shouldn't be walking around with their heads down in sorrow and defeat wondering, "My God, what are we ever going to do? How are we ever going to get out of this!" No, when God's favor is on you, you should be walking with an uplifted face. You should walk with a countenance of joy on you! Even though all of hell's power has broken loose in your life, you are confident that your God will deliver you. Amen.

When you walk in the favor of God, you don't bow down to Satan's pressure any more. He is no longer your master. It's time to stand up and tell him, "You're talking to someone who is highly favored of God. Are you trying to tell me this is impossible? Just watch. I love it when you say, 'impossible' because you don't know who you are talking to. I have favor with God. The favor of God surrounds me like a shield. It goes before me. It causes me to have a countenance of joy even in adversity. It enables me to laugh at my enemy because I know his day is coming."

We need to expect to increase in it, and have a positive attitude that every adversity will be turned into victory because the favor of God is upon us and we cannot be defeated.

Exceeding Favor

Recently as I was studying the favor of God, I found that we have the right to walk in this favor above and beyond what I had even imagined. So far, you've seen a glimpse of what God's favor can produce in your life, but what you are about to read is going to broaden your thinking so much that you can't help but get excited.

Ephesians 2:7 says,

That in the ages to come he might shew the exceeding riches of his grace in his kindness toward us through Christ Jesus.

He says that in the ages to come He wants to show (or demonstrate or manifest) the exceeding riches of His grace. In other words, He wants to show us something that is tangible, something that you can see. The word "exceeding" in itself takes us out of the norm. "Exceeding" always expresses "above and beyond." This is going to be beyond anything you've ever experienced before. To whom does He want to show this? Those who are in Christ Jesus. He's talking to you. God's going to show the exceeding riches of His grace to you.

The Amplified says it this way:

He did this that He might clearly demonstrate through the ages to come the immeasurable (limitless, surpassing) riches of His free grace (His unmerited favor) in kindness and goodness of heart toward us in Christ Jesus.

Notice three words, "immeasurable, limitless and surpassing." Paul is saying, "I have experienced a level of God's grace, but in the ages to come, the grace that the last days church (us) will experience will surpass the grace that my generation is experiencing."

In order that in the coming ages, He might show the incomparable riches of His grace, expressed in His kindness to us in Christ Jesus.

So, we're going to experience His grace in ways that are surpassing, incomparable, limitless, and immeasurable! Obviously, this verse speaks of leaving the norm and moving into the realm of the "above and beyond."

The dictionary defines immeasurable as boundless, vast, immense. How far is vast? It is beyond anything we could possibly ask or think. Limitless is defined as "infinite." The word surpassing is defined as "going beyond the limits, going beyond your range or your capacity."

In the Old testament, when you see the word "exceed, exceeding, or exceedingly," it means "abundance, overflowing," but it also means "to hang over."
Exceeding also implies "not enough room to hold." That explains why David said, "My cup runneth over!" He will pour out blessings that there will not be room enough to contain it all.

You and I are about to experience the immeasurable, limitless, surpassing riches of His grace and His kindness.
Kindness always denotes favor. If you were to ask someone, "Would you do a favor for me?" And they replied, "Sure. What do you need?" What is that an expression of? Kindness. It also expresses covenant relationship.

God is kind. He is full of compassion. He said that in the ages to come we will experience the immeasurable, surpassing, limitless expressions of His grace, His kindness and His favor.

The best way I know how to describe it is in comparison with my daughters and my grandchildren. I have two daughters, and while they were growing up, they experienced my grace. On the other hand, I have two grandsons and one granddaughter, but they experience my limitless, immeasurable, surpassing grace!

In fact, my daughters ask me often, "Daddy, why do you let the grandkids do what you didn't let us do?" And I say, "You were under grace, but they are under surpassing grace!"

Now, I met all of their needs. I was kind to them. I proved my love to them. In fact, they wrote me notes all the time saying, "You're the best Daddy in the whole world." But my grandkids are over in that immeasurable, surpassing and limitless arena. They don't even have to ask for it. It's waiting for them when they come! Do you understand what I'm saying?

That's what God is about to do with you and me! Hallelujah! He's going to show us favor like no other generation has ever experienced.

The Message translation says, "He's going to shower us with blessings." Do you know what that means? No more "mercy drops," as religious people often say, but showers of kindness and grace! Grace has been defined as "unmerited favor." But another definition which I really like is "the ability of God coming on you enabling you to do what you can't do for yourself!" Isn't that good? For by grace are ye saved. I couldn't do that myself. It took grace. That's God's ability to do what I can't do in myself. So, let's tie that definition into Ephesians 2:7:

He did this that He might clearly demonstrate through the ages to come the immeasurable (limitless, surpassing) riches of His free grace (His unmerited favor) in kindness and goodness of heart toward us in Christ Jesus.

This tells me that you and I will be able to accomplish things we have not been able to accomplish in the past. The ability of God will come on us to do what we've never been able to do before.

God is enabling the church to experience a set time of favor and grace. That doesn't mean we won't have opposition! No! We'll have opposition. We'll still have a Devil to deal with. But we're going to experience greater victories than we've ever experienced before! It means that doors that have never opened to you before will begin to open now.

Luke 4:19 (Amplified version) says,

To proclaim the accepted and acceptable year of the Lord— the day when salvation and the free favors of God profusely abound.

In other words, God is saying when His favors profusely abound in your life, then you will go beyond the limitations that have been there in the past, and you'll break barriers that you've never been able to break before.

If you believe that you are a part of the last days church, then get ready for God's favor to profusely abound as never before. Lay hold on what belongs to you as one who is in Christ Jesus. Expect freedom in every area. Expect restoration and increase.

The dictionary also defines the word favor as: "to endorse, to support, to assist, to make easier, to provide with advantages, to show special privileges, or to be featured."

Would you like a few of your faith projects to be a little easier? I didn't say you wouldn't have to use your faith. You're going to use your faith throughout eternity! But wouldn't it be wonderful if the sowing and reaping process was accelerated and things got easier?

In fact, the Spirit of God told me to right this down, and I encourage you to read it and keep it before you as encouragement: "Begin to expect Me to show up in everything you do and everywhere you go so I can support you, endorse you, assist you, make things easier, provide you with advantages, and grant special privileges."

I receive that! Now, you can read this book and say, "Wasn't that a nice little book Brother Jerry wrote on favor," or you can receive this into your spirit, and lay hold of it until it becomes such a reality in your life that you begin walking in God's divine favor every day. Remember you get exactly what you expect. Jesus said, "Be it done unto you according to your faith."

My faith is going for this. My faith is going to lay hold of this, praise God. I've already experienced the favor of God in my life but now I'm ready for the "surpassing, immeasurable, limitless" favor of God like never before.

What does it mean "to be featured?" To feature implies "to give special prominence." That's what favor will do. We see an example of this in Joshua 10. Remember Joshua and the children of Israel are engaged in warfare, and it says,

Then spake Joshua to the Lord in the day when the Lord delivered up the Amorites before the children of Israel, and he said in the sight of Israel, Sun, stand thou still upon Gibeon; and thou, Moon, in the valley of Ajalon.

And the sun stood still, and the moon stayed, until the people had avenged themselves upon their enemies. Is not this written in the book of Jasher? So the sun stood still in the midst of heaven and hasted not to go down about a whole day.

And there was no day like that before it or after it, that the Lord hearkened (featured, favored)
unto the voice of a man: for the Lord fought for Israel.

Joshua 10:12-14:

When God hearkened to Joshua's words, He favored him. There had never been a day like that before where God so "featured" one of His own. Can you imagine that? Talk about favor. When was the last time you told the sun to stand still because you needed more daylight? When was the last time you told the moon, "Be still. Don't move," and it obeyed you?

God allowed Joshua to experience His favor, His power, and His ability like no man had ever experienced before. You're going to have days where you'll hear yourself say, "I've never seen a day like this!" And this time you won't be referring to bad days, you'll be referring to good days!

God wants us to begin to expect Him to show up everywhere we go and in everything we do. Why? So He can endorse, support, assist, make easier, provide with advantages, grant special privileges, feature and give us special prominence.

Can you imagine how exciting your life will become when that starts happening? That's favor. God wants to make your life better. If there is any one thing believers need right now, it is deliverance from being stressed out. So many Christians are stressed out. They are on the verge of "burn out." Well, God wants to make your life easier. That doesn't mean a free ride. That doesn't mean you can just sit back and coast along, but it does mean that God will get involved in what you are doing and make life easier.

He wants to grant you special privileges and special advantages. He wants to feature you and give you special prominence. So, if you can imagine that kind of favor manifesting in your life, it is going to cause your life to become a tremendous adventure in faith.

The key to walking in this kind of favor is found in James 4:6 ...God resisteth the proud, but giveth grace unto the humble. The more you acknowledge that without Him you are nothing, the more of this kind of grace and favor you will experience.

Don't try to make these things happen yourself. All you'll do is tie God's hands. Just stay humble before God and allow that favor and grace to be given to you by reason of the pureness of your heart and humility.

I believe that God truly desires to demonstrate this kind of favor which He calls "immeasurable, limitless and surpassing" to a people who will no longer lean to the arm of the flesh but simply trust Him. It's time for God's favor to profusely abound, so let it happen and keep praising Him for it.

Fullness of Favor

God is saving the best for last. We are the ones who are going to experience the favor of God in its fullness. Get ready because there are going to be some changes around your house—favor is coming!

Thou shalt arise, and have mercy upon Zion: for the time to favour her, yea, the set time, is come.

Psalm 102:13

Notice the Psalmist said the set time is come. I believe that this is a key phrase. A "set time" would indicate that God's already programmed it in and no devil, or man, or government can change it. It is a set time. Notice what this "set time" is for:

Favor to come upon Zion. Zion is always symbolic of the church. In other words, there is a set time for favor to come upon the church like it has never experienced before. Please understand that the Psalm is prophetic.

Remember we're reading the words of a prophet, not just a king, nor just a psalmist. He's seeing into the future.

Verse 15 says,

So the heathen shall fear the name of the Lord and all the kings of the earth thy glory.

Now look at what Isaiah prophesied concerning the church in the future.

Arise, shine; for thy light is come, and the glory of the Lord is risen upon thee. For behold, the darkness shall cover the earth, and gross darkness the people: but the Lord shall arise upon thee, and his glory shall be seen upon thee. And the Gentiles shall come to thy light, and kings to the brightness of thy rising.

He talks about the glory of God coming upon the church and it actually will be seen on us. When will this happen? When the world is in its darkest hour, the Church will be at its brightest.

Verse 16 pinpoints the time frame:

When the Lord shall build up Zion, [or the church] he shall appear in his glory.

In other words, He's saying, "Before the appearing of the Lord, there will be a 'set time' of favor that the church will experience!" This "set time" will precede His appearing! And guess what? It's already happening! So, we're in it right now. The "ages to come" that Paul spoke about in Ephesians 2:7 have come. Therefore, we should expect the favor of God on us like never before.

Favor Makes Wealth

Lift up thine eyes round about, and see: all they gather themselves together, they come to thee:

Isaiah 60:1-3

thy sons shall come from far, and thy daughters shall be nursed at thy side.
Then thou shall see, and flow together, and thine heart shall fear, and be enlarged; because the abundance of the sea shall be converted unto thee, the forces of the Gentiles shall come unto thee.

Isaiah 60:4,5

In the Hebrew, the word "forces" is translated "wealth." Wealth is associated or connected to favor. If you study your Bible, you'll see that many who walked in the favor of God experienced financial blessings as well. Favor produces wealth.

We know that God has prophesied that a financial inversion will take place in the earth before the appearing of the Lord Jesus, and that the wealth of the sinner has been laid up for the just. So, if this "set time" of favor has come, then the church can anticipate greater wealth and finances. It will be experienced by those who are faithful and living right-eously according to the Word of God. If you are one of those, then you are a candidate for greater finances than you've ever experienced before in your life. Of course this only applies to tithers. If you aren't a tither, then He's certainly not going to cause this financial inversion to come on you. But on the other hand, if you are a tither, then get ready because He's going to pile it on those He can trust!

I want you to see a pattern for this in 2 Chronicles 1:12 when Solomon was given the assignment to build the temple.

Wisdom and knowledge is granted unto thee; and I will give thee riches, and wealth, and honour, (or favor) such as none of the kings have had that have been before thee, neither shall there any after thee have the like.

God is saying, "I'm about to put favor on you like no one before you has ever walked in."

And the king made silver and gold at Jerusalem as plenteous as stones... 2 Chronicles 1:15

Can you imagine having as much gold and silver as you have gravel in your driveway?

Send me therefore a man cunning to work in gold... Send me also cedar trees, fir trees...

2 Chronicles 2:7,8

In other words, during a time of favor, God supplies everything you need to get the job done.

Even to prepare me timber in abundance: for the house which I am about to build shall be wonderful great.

2 Chronicles 2:9

Do you need timber in abundance? I do! We're building, building, building and we need timber in abundance. Are you believing for a house? Then, you need timber in abundance. Well, favor produces it!

And we will cut wood out of Lebanon, as much as thou shalt need...

2 Chronicles 2:16

We're not going to "barely get by" any more. We're not going to have to cut any corners. No, when favor comes, you'll have "as much as thou shalt need."

Thus all the work that Solomon made for the house of the Lord was finished...

2 Chronicles 5:1

And the next thing that happens is the Lord appears in His glory:

It came even to pass, as the trumpeters and singers were as one, to make one sound to be heard in praising and thanking the Lord: and when they lifted up their voice with the trumpets and cymbals and instruments of musick and praised the Lord, saying, For he is good; for his mercy endureth for ever: that then the house was filled with a cloud, even the house of the Lord;

So that the priests could not stand to minister by reason of the cloud for the glory of the Lord had filled the house of God.

2 Chronicles 5:13,14

... the time to favour her, yea, the set time, is come.

...When the Lord shall build up Zion, he shall appear in his glory.

Psalm 102:13,16

Notice what precedes the appearing of the Lord: a "set time of favor." We just read about a pattern for that when Solomon built the temple. Notice God granted him honor and favor and with it came riches, wealth and honor. Not only that, but with it came the right people, all that he needed, abundance, plenty, expertise, quality, talent, and anointing. I submit to you that we are in that set time and that's what we can expect.

Can you imagine how exciting this is going to be as we lay hold of it and begin to walk in it? God is saving the best for last. Now, I want to give you 10 major benefits that I've discovered from the Word of God to those who walk in God's divine favor. These are benefits you can expect when the favor of God is on your life.

Study each of these carefully and begin to confess them everyday. God confirms His Word when we are bold to declare it.

Favor Creates Promotion.

But the Lord was with Joseph, and shewed him mercy, and gave him favour in the sight of the keeper of the prison.

Genesis 39:21

Favor produces restoration of everything that the enemy has stolen from you.

And I will give this people favour in the sight of the Egyptians: and it shall come to pass, that, when ye go, ye shall not go empty. Exodus 3:21

Favor produces honor in the midst of your adversaries.

And the Lord gave the people favour in the sight of the Egyptians. Moreover the man Moses was very great in the land of Egypt, in the sight Pharaoh's servants, and in the sight of the people. Exodus 11:3

Favor produces increased assets, especially in the area of real estate.

And of Naphtali he said, O Naphtali, satisfied with favour, and full with the blessing of the Lord, possess thou the west and the south. Deuteronomy 33:23

Favor produces great victories in the midst of great impossibilities.

For it was of the Lord to harden their hearts, that they should come against Israel in battle, that he might destroy them utterly, and that they might have no favour, but that he might destroy them, as the Lord commanded Moses. Joshua 11:20

Favor produces recognition, even when you seem the least likely to receive it.

And, Saul sent to Jesse, saying, Let David, I pray thee, stand before me; for he hath found favour in my sight. I Samuel 16:22

Favor produces prominence and preferential treatment.

And the king loved Esther above all the women, and she obtained grace and favour in his sight more than all the virgins; so that he set the royal crown upon her head, and made her queen instead of Vashti. Esther 2:17

Favor produces petitions granted even by ungodly civil

If I have found favour in the sight of the king, and if it please the king to grant my petition, and to perform my request, let the king and Haman come to the banquet that I shall prepare for them, and I will do tomorrow as the king hath said. Esther 5:8

Favor causes policies, rules, regulations and laws, to be on your side.

And said, If it please the king, and if I have found favour in his sight, and the thing seem right before the king, and I be pleasing in his eyes, let it be written to reverse the letters devised by Haman the son, of Hammedatha the Agagite, which he wrote to destroy the Jews which are in all the king's provinces. Esther 8:5

Favor produces battles won which you won't even fight because God will fight them for you.

For they got not the land in possession by their own sword, neither did their own arm save them: but thy right hand, and thine arm, and the light of thy countenance, because thou hadst a favour unto them. Psalm 44:3

Favor to Know Jesus Heart's

If you delight yourself in the Lord, He will give you the desires of your heart. Psalms 37:4

I've found out that favor will work, not only in spiritual things, but it will work in producing the desires of your heart. I discovered that the desires of your heart are very dear to the heart of the Father, particularly, if your lifestyle is pleasing to Him. When your lifestyle is pleasing to Him, then your desires will line up with His will. Your desires aren't going to be sinful or something that is out of character for a lifestyle which is pleasing to God.

If you were to die today, where would you spend eternity? If you have accepted Jesus Christ as your personal Lord and Savior, you can be assured that when you die, you will go directly into the presence of God in Heaven. If you have not accepted Jesus as your personal Lord and Savior, is there any reason why you can't make Jesus the Lord of your life right now? Please pray this prayer out loud, and as you do, pray with a sincere and trusting heart, and you will be born again.

Dear God in Heaven,

I come to you in the Name of Jesus to receive salvation and eternal life. I believe that Jesus is Your Son. I believe that He died on the cross for my sins, and that you raised Him from the dead. I receive Jesus now into my heart and make Him the Lord of my life. Jesus, come into my heart. I welcome you as my Lord and Savior. Father, I believe Your Word that says I am now saved. I confess with my mouth that I am saved and born again. I am now a child of God.

Joseph's Keys to Favor

The life of Joseph is a great study on God's favor and success. His story is a classic example of how someone can face unbelievable rejection and setbacks and still come out on top with God's favor. I'm sure you remember the story.

As a young boy, Joseph was sold by his own brothers into slavery (Gen 37). Can you imagine the horrible rejection and hurt that an event like that could produce? I'm sure that Joseph was tempted to be bitter just like anyone would. Yet, when you read the whole story, there's no mention of bitterness or a desire for revenge.

In fact, it's quite the opposite. Joseph seems to have risen above the hurt through His faith in God's destiny for his life. The Bible says that when his brothers sold him, the slave traders put him in chains and took him down to Egypt (Gen 39 / Ps 105:17-22). There, he was sold again and ended up in Potiphar's house. At that horrible time in his life, look at what Genesis 39:2-4 says about Joseph:

"And the Lord was with Joseph, and he was a prosperous man; and he was in the house of his master the Egyptian. And his master saw that the Lord was with him and that the Lord made all that he did to prosper in his hand. And Joseph found FAVOR in his sight, and he served him; and he made him overseer over his house and all that he had put into his hand."

Keep in mind that this was said of Joseph when he was a slave and own absolutely nothing. Prosperous? Favor? This one passage alone confirms that God's view of prosperity and success is far different than the world's view. In God's mind, "prosperity" is all about who you are on the inside, not what you have on the outside. God looked upon Joseph's faith and attitude and called him "prosperous." And because he was prosperous on the inside, it was just a matter of time until he experienced God's favor and blessing on the outside. Never forget that prosperity is first and foremost who you are on the inside.

Revelation of Favor

In the Name of Jesus, I am the righteousness of God. Therefore, I am entitled to covenant kindness and covenant favor. The favor of God is among the righteous. The favor of God surrounds the righteous. Therefore, it surrounds me everywhere I go and in everything I do. I expect the favor of God to be in full manifestation in my life.

Never again will I be without the favor of God. It rests richly upon me. It profusely abounds in me. I am a part of the generation that is experiencing God's favor immeasurably, limitlessly, and surpassingly. Therefore, favor produces supernatural increase, promotion, restoration, honor, increased assets, greater victories, recognition, prominence, preferential treatment, petitions granted, policies and rules changed, and battles won in which I do not have to fight.

The favor of God is on me and goes before. Therefore, my life will never be the same. This is the time of God's favor in my life. That is the favor of God. In Jesus' name, Amen.

Scripture References:

II Corinthians 9:8 Exodus 12:35-36 Genesis 39:21 Luke 2:52 Deuteronomy 33:23 Esther 8:5

Esther 5:8 Psalms 44:3 Psalms 102:13

- Pray that the spirit of favor will come to past in all areas of your life.

- Receive the favor of God from all your associates, employees and customers.
- Declare that everything you lay your hands on will carry the mark of God's approved abundance and favor.
- Thank God for the favor of God upon your life family and home.
- Thank God for clothing you with glory and honor.
- Praise God for honoring His word in your life and the favor it releases on your life.
- Thank God because His presence will radiate joy in your life all the time.
- Thank God that He causes us to triumph through the Lord Jesus Christ.
- Pray God that the kindness of the Lord will be upon you.
- Confess that you will be the head and not the tail according to God's word.
- Confess that you are above only.
- Pray for supernatural increase in all areas of life.
- Ask God to bless you with abundance of supernatural grace.
- Pray for a supernatural flow of favor into your life uninterrupted.
- Pray that as you walk with the Lord that you will always experience His favor.
- Receive the favor of understanding and supernatural learning ability in the name of Jesus.
- Pray that you will receive a new baptism of the spirit of grace and favor.
- Pray that you will constantly walk in favor with God and man.

- Confess that you are designed for favor, goodness and blessing, and predestined to make them a way of life daily.

Financial Favor

1.   Pray that the Lord will give the Faith Embassy International Ministries -Revelation Church- congregation a giver's heart so that they may increase, according to His promise, and accomplish Gods will for their life.

2.   Praise the Lord by faith, for the miracle of debt cancellation for Faith Embassy International Ministries - Revelation Church- and congregation.

3.   Ask the Lord for the grace and blessing that will make you a lender and not a borrower.

4.   Declare by faith that the rest of the Faith Embassy International Ministries -Revelation Church- congregation shall not be in struggle but prosperity.

5.   Pray that harvest would meet in your life.

6.   Pray that the Lord will open up Faith Embassy International Ministries -Revelation Church- congregation's eyes to see the good ground of ministry in which to sow your gifts of finance

7.   I decree financial increase that will transform the congregation of Faith Embassy International Ministries - Revelation Church- from struggle to abundance.

8.   Pray for the divine ability to be a kingdom promoter using your finances for the ministry.

9.   Prophesy into the congregation of Faith Embassy International Ministries -Revelation Church- future a lifestyle of continuous blessing and favor.

10.   Pray that despite the attack of the enemy it will all result in promotion and the favor of God on their lives.

11.   By faith declare that because we trust in God we will not lack any good thing.

12. In the face of financial set back, we declare to the Faith Embassy International Ministries -Revelation Church- congregation that God's plan and covenant of blessing shall stand.

13. Decree that our seed shall bring only abundance and they shall not beg.

14. Speak to their mountain and command it to turn to a land of wealth.

15. We believe and confess that the congregation of Faith Embassy International Ministries -Revelation Church- are already loaded with His benefits.

16. Possess a future of abundant wealth for the congregation of Faith Embassy International Ministries -Revelation Church- and their children in the name of Jesus.

17. We pray for wisdom to be a good steward of God's provision.

18. We as a congregation receive the creativity for the creation of wealth in the name of Lord.

19. Ask God for the grace and strength to retain the blessing He is bringing into their life.

20. We ask the Lord for the boldness to possess the wealth of the wicked.

21. We ask the Lord to teach us how to profit in the things you have set our mind to do.

22. We pray that every step we take will result in blessing and increase.

23. We ask the Lord to increase the congregation's zeal and devotion despite financial blessing.

Insight of Favor

In reading this, then, you will be able to understand my insight into the mystery of Christ, Ephesians 3:4

I do not want you to be ignorant of this mystery, brothers, so that you will not be conceited: A hardening in part has come to Israel, until the full number of the Gentiles has come in. Romans 11:25

Now to Him who is able to strengthen you by my gospel and by the proclamation of Jesus Christ, according to the revelation of the mystery concealed for ages past, Romans 16:25

Although I am not a polished speaker, I am certainly not lacking in knowledge. We have made this clear to you in every way possible.   2   Corinthians   11:6

that is, the mystery made known to me by revelation, as I have already written briefly. Ephesians 3:3

Favor-Key #1 – Prosperity is first and foremost who you are on the "inside" (in your mind, heart, and character) and not what you have on the outside. God already sees you as a winner.

Favor-Key #2 - If you are a prosperous person on the inside then it's just be a matter of time until you will see things change on the outside (if you refuse to give up). Hold on to your faith.

Favor-Key #3 - The experiential side of God's favor is linked to how you respond to adversities, setbacks, offenses, and temptations. Keep trusting God.

Favor-Key #4 - The principle of "working as unto the Lord" activates God's favor and blessing. It's the way you can express your faith each and every day regardless of what kind of work you do.

Foundation of Favor

However, as it is written: "No eye has seen, no ear has heard, no mind has conceived what God has prepared for those who love him"-1 Cor 2:9NIV

Every genuine lover of God is a wonder on earth. Prov 23:26

26 My son, give me your heart and let your eyes keep to my ways, NIV

- Give God your heart and you make marks on earth.

- Give your heart to loving God and you will end up a living wonder on the earth. Mark 12:30-31 30 Love the Lord your God with all your heart and with all your soul and with all your mind and with all your strength.' 31 The second is this: `Love your neighbor as yourself.' There is no commandment greater than these." NIV

King Solomon showed his love for God by walking in obedience to God just as his father King David did, and that brought him favour from God.

1 Kings 3:3

3 Solomon showed his love for the LORD by walking according to the statutes of his father David, except that he offered sacrifices and burned incense on the high places. NIV

1 Kings 4:30-34

30 Solomon's wisdom was greater than the wisdom of all the men of the East, and greater than all the wisdom of Egypt. 31 He was wiser than any other man, including Ethan the Ezrahite-wiser than Heman, Calcol and Darda, the sons of Mahol. And his fame spread to all the surrounding nations. 32 He spoke three thousand proverbs and his songs numbered a thousand and five. 33 He described plant life, from the cedar of Lebanon to the hyssop that grows out of walls. He also taught about animals and birds, reptiles and fish. 34 Men of all nations came to listen to Solomon's wisdom, sent by all the kings of the world, who had heard of his wisdom. NIV

Song 8:6
6 Place me like a seal over your heart, like a seal on your arm; for love is as strong as death, its jealousy unyielding as the grave. It burns like blazing fire, like a mighty flame. NIV

Daniel 3:1-28; Daniel 6: 1-23
- Love is as strong as death. Because their love for God was so strong, they were ready to
give up their lives for God.
- Love never fails. Everything in the kingdom works around it.

Faith works by love Gal 5:6
6 For in Christ Jesus neither circumcision nor uncircumcision has any value. The only thing that counts is faith expressing itself through love. NIV

Faith works with revelation, and revelation works through love. Without love, nothing works in the kingdom. If you don't have love for God, you won't receive revelation (insight into scriptures and things of the Spirit), and without revelation, there can be no strong and productive faith, and without faith, there will be no breakthroughs, miracles and supernatural manifestations.

1 Cor 13:2-3

3 If I give all I possess to the poor and surrender my body to the flames, but have not love, I gain nothing. NIV

Your supernatural breakthrough is by engaging the law of love. Job 13:15

15 Though he slay me, yet will I hope in him; I will surely defend my ways to his face. NIV

Job 1:1-3

1:1 In the land of Uz there lived a man whose name was Job. This man was blameless and upright; he feared God and shunned evil. 2 He had seven sons and three daughters, 3 and he owned seven thousand sheep, three thousand camels, five hundred yoke of oxen and five hundred donkeys, and had a large number of servants. He was the greatest man among all the people of the East. NIV

anointed with oil of gladness. Ps 45:7

7 You love righteousness and hate wickedness; therefore God, your God, has set you above your companions by anointing you with the oil of joy. NIV

- Your level of love determines your level of anointing. Ps 89:20-24

20 I have found David my servant; with my sacred oil I have anointed him. 21 My hand will sustain him; surely my arm will

strengthen him. 22 No enemy will subject him to tribute; no wicked man will oppress him. 23 I will crush his foes before him and strike down his adversaries. 24 My faithful love will be with him, and through my name his horn will be exalted. NIV

Ps 45:8

8 All your robes are fragrant with myrrh and aloes and cassia; from palaces adorned with ivory the music of the strings makes you glad. NIV

- The anointing attracts favour. Gen 27:27

27 So he went to him and kissed him. When Isaac caught the smell of his clothes, he blessed him and said, "Ah, the smell of my son is like the smell of a field that the LORD has blessed. NIV

Luke 2:52

52 And Jesus grew in wisdom and stature, and in favour with God and men. NIV

Luke   2:40
40 And the child grew and became strong; he was filled with wisdom, and the grace of God was upon him. NIV
- The stronger the anointing the greater the favour. The hotter your love the greater the anointing.
- The love for God produces the anointing, and the anointing produces the favour.
- Every provision of the kingdom leaves you with a responsibility to take delivery of them. Favour is not free. It has to be entreated. It has to be bought into. Your deep love for God

gives you access to it. Your love motivated generous and sacrificial giving provokes favor.

5. anointed with oil of gladness.

Ps 45:7
7 You love righteousness and hate wickedness; therefore God, your God, has set you above your companions by anointing you with the oil of joy. NIV

• Your level of love determines your level of anointing. Ps 89:20-24
20 I have found David my servant; with my sacred oil I have anointed him. 21 My hand will sustain him; surely my arm will strengthen him. 22 No enemy will subject him to tribute; no wicked man will oppress him. 23 I will crush his foes before him and strike down his adversaries. 24 My faithful love will be with him, and through my name his horn will be exalted. NIV

Ps 45:8
8 All your robes are fragrant with myrrh and aloes and cassia; from palaces adorned with ivory the music of the strings makes you glad. NIV

• The anointing attracts favour. Gen 27:27
27 So he went to him and kissed him. When Isaac caught the smell of his clothes, he blessed him and said, "Ah, the smell of my son is like the smell of a field that the LORD has blessed. NIV

Luke 2:52
52 And Jesus grew in wisdom and stature, and in favour with God and men. NIV

Luke 2:40
40 And the child grew and became strong; he was filled with wisdom, and the grace of God was upon him. NIV
- The stronger the anointing the greater the favour. The hotter your love the greater the anointing.
- The love for God produces the anointing, and the anointing produces the favour.
- Every provision of the kingdom leaves you with a responsibility to take delivery of them. Favour is not free. It has to be entreated. It has to be bought into. Your deep love for God gives you access to it. Your love motivated generous and sacrificial giving provokes favour.

5. Love gives you access to blessings.

Gen 49:25
25 because of your father's God, who helps you, because of the Almighty, who blesses you with blessings of the heavens above, blessings of the deep that lies below, blessings of the breast and womb. NIV
- Your love for God entitles you to his blessings upon your life. Isa 65:8

8 This is what the LORD says: "As when juice is still found in a cluster of grapes and men say, `Don't destroy it, there is yet some good in it,' so will I do in behalf of my servants; I will not destroy them all. NIV
- These blessings are proclaimed through human lips.
- Your duty is to honour your father.

Ex 20:12
12 "Honor your father and your mother, so that you may live long in the land the LORD your God is giving you. NIV

Eph 6:2
2 "Honor your father and mother"-which is the first commandment with a promise- NIV
•   Honour your fathers and they will bless you. Love your fathers and their blessings will make you great.
•   To honour your father is to respect, listen to and give gifts to him.

Three parental roots:

1. Parental root in God. John 1:12
12 Yet to all who received him, to those who believed in his name, he gave the right to become children of God- NIV

Mal 1:6

6 "A son honors his father, and a servant his master. If I am a father, where is the honor due me? If I am a master, where is the respect due me?" says the LORD Almighty. "It is you, O priests, who show contempt for my name. "But you ask, `How have we shown contempt for your name?' NIV

2.   Parental root in spiritual fathers. 1 Cor 4:15

15 Even though you have ten thousand guardians in Christ, you do not have many fathers, for in Christ Jesus I became your father   through   the   gospel. NIV

2 Kings 2:12

12 Elisha saw this and cried out, "My father! My father! The chariots and horsemen of Israel!" And Elisha saw him no more.

Then he took hold of his own clothes and tore them apart.
NIV

2 Kings 6:21
21 When the king of Israel saw them, he asked Elisha, "Shall I kill them, my father? Shall I kill them?"
NIV

3.   Parental root in biological fathers
God blessings will give you your place no matter where you are.
Love for God is all that leads the way to all these blessings.

Access to Blessings & Favor

Gen 49:25

25 because of your father's God, who helps you, because of the Almighty, who blesses you with blessings of the heavens above, blessings of the deep that lies below, blessings of the breast and womb. NIV

- Your love for God entitles you to his blessings upon your life. Isa 65:8

8 This is what the LORD says: "As when juice is still found in a cluster of grapes and men say, `Don't destroy it, there is yet some good in it,' so will I do in behalf of my servants; I will not destroy them all. NIV

- These blessings are proclaimed through human lips.

- Your duty is to honour your father.

Ex 20:12

12 "Honor your father and your mother, so that you may live long in the land the LORD your God is giving you. NIV

Eph 6:2

2 "Honor your father and mother"-which is the first commandment with a promise- NIV

- Honour your fathers and they will bless you. Love your fathers and their blessings will make you great.

- To honour your father is to respect, listen to and give gifts to him.

Three parental roots:

1. Parental root in God. John 1:12

12 Yet to all who received him, to those who believed in his name, he gave the right to become children of God- NIV

Mal 1:6

6 "A son honors his father, and a servant his master. If I am a father, where is the honor due me? If I am a master, where is the respect due me?" says the LORD Almighty. "It is you, O priests, who show contempt for my name. "But you ask, `How have we shown contempt for your name?' NIV

2.   Parental root in spiritual fathers. 1 Cor 4:15

15 Even though you have ten thousand guardians in Christ, you do not have many fathers, for in Christ Jesus I became your father   through   the   gospel. NIV

2 Kings 2:12

12 Elisha saw this and cried out, "My father! My father! The chariots and horsemen of Israel!" And Elisha saw him no more.

Then he took hold of his own clothes and tore them apart. NIV

2 Kings 6:21

21 When the king of Israel saw them, he asked Elisha, "Shall I kill them, my father? Shall I kill them?" NIV

3.   Parental root in biological fathers

•   God blessings will give you your place no matter where you are.

•   Love for God is all that leads the way to all these blessings.

Men Who Walked with Favor

But Noah found favor in the eyes of the LORD Genesis 6:8
But the LORD was with Joseph and extended kindness to him,
and gave him favor in the sight of the chief jailer. Genesis 39:21

Then Moses said to the LORD, "See, You say to me, 'Bring
up this people!' But You Yourself have not let me know whom
You will send with me Moreover, You have said, 'I have known
you by name, and you have also found favor in My sight.'
Exodus 33:12

Now the boy Samuel was growing in stature and in favor both
with the LORD and with men. 1 Samuel 2:26

So you will find favor and good repute In the sight of God and
man. Proverbs 3:4

"For he who finds me finds life And obtains favor from the
LORD Proverbs 8:35

A good man will obtain favor from the LORD, But He will
condemn a man who devises evil. Proverbs 12:2

He who finds a wife finds a good thing And obtains favor from
the LORD. Proverbs 18:22

The angel said to her, "Do not be afraid, Mary; for you have
found favor with God. Luke 1:30

And Jesus kept increasing in wisdom and stature, and in **favor** with God and men. Luke 2:52

"David found **favor** in God's sight, and asked that he might find a dwelling place for the God of Jacob. Acts 7:46

For You are the glory of their strength, And by Your **favor** our horn is exalted. Psalm 89:17

"Foreigners will build up your walls, And their kings will minister to you; For in My wrath I struck you, And in My **favor** I have had compassion on you. Isaiah 60:10

Unstoppable Favor

"For the Lord God is a sun and a shield; THE LORD WILL GIVE FAVOR and glory; No good thing will He withhold from those who walk uprightly" Psalm 84:11

"So it was, when the king's command and decree were heard, and when many young women were gathered at Shushan the citadel, under the custody of Hegai, that Esther also was taken to the king's palace, into the care of Hegai the custodian of the women. Now the young woman pleased him, AND SHE OBTAINED HIS FAVOR; so he readily gave beauty preparations to her, with her allowance. Then seven choice maidservants were provided for her from the king's palace, and he moved her and her maidservants to the BEST place in the house of the women." Esther 2:8-9

"when the king saw queen Esther standing in the court, SHE FOUND FAVOR IN HIS SIGHT, and the king held out to Esther the golden sceptre that was in his hand." Esther 5:2

"Now when the turn came for Esther the daughter of Abihail the uncle of Mordecai, who had taken her as his daughter, to go in to the king, she requested nothing but what Hagai the king's eunuch, the custodian of the women, advised. AND ESTHER OBTAINED FAVOR IN THE SIGHT OF ALL WHO SAW HER. So Esther was taken to the king Ahasuerus, into his royal palace, in the tenth month which is the month of Tebeth, in the seventh year of his reign. The king loved Esther more than all the women, and SHE OBTAINED GRACE AND FAVOR IN

HIS SIGHT MORE THAN ALL THE VIRGINS; so he set the royal crown upon her head and made her queen instead of Vashti." Esther 2:15-17

"THE LORD was with Joseph and showed him mercy, and HE GAVE HIM FAVOR in the sight of the keeper of the prison. And the keeper of the prison committed to Joseph's hand all the prisoners who were in the prison; whatever they did there, it was his doing. The keeper of the prison did not look into anything that was under Joseph's authority, because the Lord was with him; and whatever he did, the Lord made it prosper" Genesis 39:21-23

Now when the turn of Esther, the daughter of Abihail the uncle of Mordecai, who had taken her for his daughter, was come to go in unto the king, she required nothing but what Hegai the king's chamberlain, the keeper of the women, appointed. And Esther obtained favour in the sight of all them that looked upon her. So Esther was taken unto king Ahasuerus into his house royal in the tenth month, which is the month Tebeth, in the seventh year of his reign. And the king loved Esther above all the women, and she obtained grace and favour in his sight more than all the virgins; so that he set the royal crown upon her head, and made her queen instead of Vashti. Esther 2:15-17

And he lift up his eyes and looked, and, lo, three men stood by him: and when he saw them, he ran to meet them from the tent door, and bowed himself toward the ground, And said, My Lord, if now I have found favour in thy sight, pass not away, I pray thee, from thy servant: Let a little water, I pray you, be fetched, and wash your feet, and rest yourselves under the tree: And I will fetch a morsel of bread, and comfort ye your hearts;

after that ye shall pass on: for therefore are ye come to your servant. And they said, So do, as thou hast said. Genesis 18:2-5 And I will stretch out my hand, and smite Egypt with all my wonders which I will do in the midst of it: and after that he will let you go. And I will give this people favor in the sight of the Egyptians: and it shall come to pass, that, when you go, you shall not go empty: But every woman shall request of her neighbor, and of her that sojourns in her house, jewels of silver, and jewels of gold, and clothing: and you shall put them upon your sons, and upon your daughters; and you shall spoil the Egyptians. Exodus 3:20-22

Judge me, O LORD my God, according to thy righteousness; and let them not rejoice over me. Let them not say in their hearts, Ah, so would we have it: let them not say, We have swallowed him up. Let them be ashamed and brought to confusion together that rejoice at mine hurt: let them be clothed with shame and dishonour that magnify themselves against me. Let them shout for joy, and be glad, that favour my righteous cause: yea, let them say continually, Let the LORD be magnified, which hath pleasure in the prosperity of his servant. And my tongue shall speak of thy righteousness and of thy praise all the day long. Psalms 35:24-28

And Joseph's master took him, and put him into the prison, a place where the king's prisoners were bound: and he was there in the prison. But the LORD was with Joseph, and showed him mercy, and gave him favor in the sight of the keeper of the prison. And the keeper of the prison committed to Joseph's hand all the prisoners that were in the prison; and whatsoever they did there, he was the doer of it. The keeper of the prison looked not to anything that was under his hand; because the LORD was with him, and that which he did, the LORD made it to prosper.

Genesis 39:20-23 o those who accepted his message were baptized, and that day about 3,000 people were added to them.

And they devoted themselves to the apostles' teaching, to the fellowship, to the breaking of bread, and to the prayers.

Then fear came over everyone, and many wonders and signs were being performed through the apostles. Now all the believers were together and held all things in common.

They sold their possessions and property and distributed the proceeds to all, as anyone had a need. Every day they devoted themselves to meeting together in the temple complex, and broke bread from house to house. They ate their food with a joyful and humble attitude, praising God and having favor with all the people. And every day the Lord added to them those who were being saved. Acts 2:41-47

Abel, on his part also brought of the firstlings of his flock and of their fat portions And the LORD had regard for Abel and for his offering; Genesis 4:4

But Noah found favor in the eyes of the LORD. Genesis 6:8

But the LORD was with Joseph and extended kindness to him, and gave him favor in the sight of the chief jailer. Genesis 39:21

God saw the sons of Israel, and God took notice of them. Exodus 2:25

Then Moses said to the LORD, "See, You say to me, 'Bring up this people!' But You Yourself have not let me know whom You will send with me Moreover, You have said, 'I have known you by name, and you have also found favor in My sight.' Exodus 33:12

Now the boy Samuel was growing in stature and in favor both with the LORD and with men. 1 Samuel 2:26

But the LORD was gracious to them and had compassion on them and turned to them because of His covenant with Abraham, Isaac, and Jacob, and would not destroy them or cast them from His presence until now. 2 Kings 13:23

Favor to Restore Life's

Job 33:26
Then he will pray to God, and He will accept him, That he may see His face with joy, And He may restore His righteousness to man.

Proverbs 3:4
So you will find favor and good repute In the sight of God and man.

Proverbs 8:35
"For he who finds me finds life And obtains favor from the LORD.

Proverbs 12:2
A good man will obtain favor from the LORD, But He will condemn a man who devises evil.

Proverbs 18:22
He who finds a wife finds a good thing And obtains favor from the LORD.

Luke 1:30
The angel said to her, "Do not be afraid, Mary; for you have found favor with God.

Luke 2:52
And Jesus kept increasing in wisdom and stature, and in favor with God and men.

Acts 7:46

"David found favor in God's sight, and asked that he might find a dwelling place for the God of Jacob.

Genesis 43:29

As he lifted his eyes and saw his brother Benjamin, his mother's son, he said, "Is this your youngest brother, of whom you spoke to me?" And he said, "May God be gracious to you, my son."

Favor to Shine

Numbers 6:25
The LORD make His face shine on you, And be gracious to you;

Psalm 31:16
Make Your face to shine upon Your servant; Save me in Your lovingkindness.

Psalm 67:1
God be gracious to us and bless us, And cause His face to shine upon us-- Selah.

Psalm 80:3
O God, restore us And cause Your face to shine upon us, and we will be saved.

Psalm 119:135
Make Your face shine upon Your servant, And teach me Your statutes.

Isaiah 33:2
O LORD, be gracious to us; we have waited for You Be their strength every morning, Our salvation also in the time of distress.

Daniel 9:17
"So now, our God, listen to the prayer of Your servant and to his supplications, and for Your sake, O Lord, let Your face shine on Your desolate sanctuary.

Psalm 89:17
For You are the glory of their strength, And by Your favor our horn is exalted.

Isaiah 30:18
Therefore the LORD longs to be gracious to you, And therefore He waits on high to have compassion on you For the LORD is a God of justice; How blessed are all those who long for Him.

Isaiah 60:10
"Foreigners will build up your walls, And their kings will minister to you; For in My wrath I struck you, And in My favor I have had compassion on you.

Isaiah 62:4 It will no longer be said to you, "Forsaken," Nor to your land will it any longer be said, "Desolate"; But you will be called, "My delight is in her," And your land, "Married"; For the LORD delights in you, And to Him your land will be married.

Rejoice in Favor

Isaiah 65:19
"I will also rejoice in Jerusalem and be glad in My people; And there will no longer be heard in her The voice of weeping and the sound of crying.

Jeremiah 32:41
"I will rejoice over them to do them good and will faithfully plant them in this land with all My heart and with all My soul.

Hosea 1:10
Yet the number of the sons of Israel Will be like the sand of the sea, Which cannot be measured or numbered; And in the place Where it is said to them, "You are not My people," It will be said to them, "You are the sons of the living God."

Amos 5:15
Hate evil, love good, And establish justice in the gate! Perhaps the LORD God of hosts May be gracious to the remnant of Joseph.

Zephaniah 3:17
"The LORD your God is in your midst, A victorious warrior He will exult over you with joy, He will be quiet in His love, He will rejoice over you with shouts of joy.

Isaiah 62:4
It will no longer be said to you, "Forsaken," Nor to your land will it any longer be said, "Desolate"; But you will be called,

"My delight is in her," And your land, "Married"; For the LORD delights in you, And to Him your land will be married.

Isaiah 30:18
Therefore the LORD longs to be gracious to you, And therefore He waits on high to have compassion on you For the LORD is a God of justice; How blessed are all those who long for Him.

Amos 5:15
Hate evil, love good, And establish justice in the gate! Perhaps the LORD God of hosts May be gracious to the remnant of Joseph.

Glorious Favor

Psalm 89:17
For You are the glory of their strength, And by Your favor our horn is exalted.

Isaiah 60:10
"Foreigners will build up your walls, And their kings will minister to you; For in My wrath I struck you, And in My favor I have had compassion on you.

Psalm 80:3
O God, restore us And cause Your face to shine upon us, and we will be saved.

Genesis 43:29
As he lifted his eyes and saw his brother Benjamin, his mother's son, he said, "Is this your youngest brother, of whom you spoke to me?" And he said, "May God be gracious to you, my son."

Numbers 6:25
The LORD make His face shine on you, And be gracious to you;

Psalm 31:16
Verse Concepts
Make Your face to shine upon Your servant; Save me in Your lovingkindness.

Psalm 67:1

God be gracious to us and bless us, And cause His face to shine upon us-- Selah.

Hebrews 13:16
And do not neglect doing good and sharing, for with such sacrifices God is pleased.

1 John 3:22
and whatever we ask we receive from Him, because we keep His commandments and do the things that are pleasing in His sight.

Voice of Favor

Matthew 3:17
and behold, a voice out of the heavens said, "This is My beloved Son, in whom I am well-pleased."

John 8:29
"And He who sent Me is with Me; He has not left Me alone, for I always do the things that are pleasing to Him."

1 Thessalonians 2:4
but just as we have been approved by God to be entrusted with the gospel, so we speak, not as pleasing men, but God who examines our hearts.

1 Thessalonians 4:1
Finally then, brethren, we request and exhort you in the Lord Jesus, that as you received from us instruction as to how you ought to walk and please God (just as you actually do walk), that you excel still more.

Proverbs 16:7
When a man's ways are pleasing to the LORD, He makes even his enemies to be at peace with him.

Hebrews 11:5
By faith Enoch was taken up so that he would not see death; AND HE WAS NOT FOUND BECAUSE GOD TOOK HIM UP; for he obtained the witness that before his being taken up he was pleasing to God.

1. Father God, I repent for myself and for those in my generational line for seeking fortune, wealth, health, and prosperity using all evil forces and powers like feng shui, fortune telling, palmistry, face reading, divination, astrology, numerology, Ouija boards, I Ching, the Chinese almanac, tarot cards, and all superstitious practices.
2. I repent for myself and for those in my generational line for seeking false destinies, magical healings, and good fortune.
3. I repent for myself and for those in my generational line for financing the worship of idols and the building of temples. I repent for all false burning of candles, oil lamps, joss sticks, paper money, paper material-assets, and incense.
4. I repent for myself and for those in my generational line for the practice of false spiritual cleansing and purification using flowers and water blessed by ungodly beings.
5. I repent for myself and for those in my generational line for the worship of all false gods and any allegiance with demons. I repent for all attempts to communicate with false idols for the purpose of prosperity, fertility, longevity, health, protection, and destiny.
6. I repent for myself and those in my generational line for consulting mediums, witch doctors, shamans, bomohs, and false healers.
7. I repent for myself and my generational line for dedicating families, possessions, land, and ourselves to other gods and idols of the land and water.
8. I repent for myself and for those in my generational line who received names for their children from leaders of false religions. I repent for myself and my generational

line for dedicating and associating our names to the dragon and other ungodly deities.

9. I repent for myself and for those in my generational line for marrying and communicating with the dead.

10. I repent for myself and for those in my generational line for worshipping the gods and goddess of the sun, moon, heavens, and stars.

11. I repent for myself and for those in my generational line who relied on the cycles of the moon for all ungodly festivals and religious activities.

12. I repent for myself and for those in my generational line who denied and spoke against Your Word and offered burnt sacrifices and flowers to the Queen of Heaven.

13. I repent for myself and for those in my generational line for discrediting You because we relied on our own prosperity, strength, and abilities, and we assumed we lacked nothing.

14. I repent for myself and for those in my generational for temple prostitution, sexual immorality, bestiality, licentiousness, and its associated vices.

15. I repent for myself and for those in my generational line for the worship and manipulation of the five elements— metals, wood, water, fire, and earth.

16. I repent for myself and for those in my generational line for practicing other forms of religion in conjunction with the Christian faith.

17. I repent for myself and for those in my generational line for all ancestral worship and all belief in reincarnation.

18. I repent for myself and for those in my generational line for all practice and worship of Buddhism, Hinduism, Taoism, Confucianism, Islam, and Shintoism.

19. I repent for myself and for those in my generational line for trading our birthright for ungodly gains.

20. I repent for myself and for those in my generational line for forsaking You Lord and Your Holy Mountain and setting a sacrificial table for fortune and filling cups with mixed wine for destiny. Lord, please remove the curse of the sword and slaughter.
21. I repent for myself and for those in my generational line for any misuse and manipulation of the prophetic gifts for self-gain and for following the ways of Balaam.
22. I repent for myself and for those in my generational line for all participation in the martial arts, tai chi, meditation, yoga, and qigong.
23. I repent for myself and for those in my generational line for bowing to and honoring our ancestors and bowing to and honoring all who called themselves masters or gurus, exalting themselves above You God, rather than honoring and bowing to You, Lord.
24. I repent for myself and for those in my generational line for all worship of animals according to Chinese zodiac signs and for trying to take on the spirit, personality, and characteristics of animals.
25. I repent for myself and for those in my generational line for binding our children to animals and gods.
26. I repent for myself and for those in my generational line for receiving impartations of skills of power from an ungodly source.
27. I repent for myself and for those in my generational line for ungodly animal expressions of the body.
28. I repent for myself and for those in my generational line who tied their coins and paper money to the signs of the zodiac and thus caused their funds to become defiled.

Favor with God and Men

And Jesus increased in wisdom and stature, and in favour with God and man". Luke 2:52

Luke 2:52 "Jesus increased in wisdom and stature, and in favour with God and men."

Definition of Favour is, "An act of kindness beyond what is due or usual." It's when you get more than you deserve: I have worked hard, but not this hard. I have been good, but not that good. I have given, but not that much! Favor!

Favor is different than "Favors". Favors are often actions designed to influence, control, and manipulate others. This is a very different thing than Divine favor! In this last USA election, we saw media giants, business people, and judges doing "favors" for politicians with an anticipated return in mind.

When this happens in government or law it is a criminal abuse of authority and it is very wrong!

Favor is when others, out of good will, seek to benefit you. "He who earnestly seeks good finds favor" (Prov 11:25) Divine favor is when God pours out His benefits on you simply because your ways have pleased Him. (Ps 103:2) When a man's ways please the Lord He causes even your enemies to favor you! (Prov 16:7)

Six Ways To Grow In Favor With Both God And Man:
1. Live your life wholeheartedly for God. "For You, O Lord, will bless the righteous: With favor You will surround him as with a shield." (Ps 5:12)

2. God is rewarder of those who diligently seek Him. (Heb11:6). Was it an accident that Pharaoh showed favor to Joseph? Or that Daniel found favor with all of the kings he served under? No! They both diligently sought the Lord, even when it wasn't to their advantage. Do it!
3. Perseverance during the pain of correction, brings long term favor. "His anger is but for a moment, His favor is for life;" (Ps 30:5). "We count them blessed who endure. You have heard of the perseverance of Job and seen the end intended by the Lord-that the Lord is very compassionate and merciful." (James 5:11) Job kept the right heart attitude and received double for his trouble!
4. Use your business to do God's business, then God makes it His business to bless your business! "Let them shout for Joy and be glad who favor my righteous cause." (Ps 35:27) Peter lent his boat to Jesus and He blessed his business big time in return. (Luke 5:1-11) It takes a commitment to being involved in God's business if you want God's favor on your business.
5. Ask for favor from God and man. "You have not because you ask not." (Jam 4:2-3) Asking your boss for an increase at the right time and in the right way can cause favor to come your way. Try making a wise appeal like Queen Esther did. (Esther 5:1-8)
6. Blessing others causes you to reap favor with others. Ruth finding favor with Boaz is a great example of this principle. (Ruth 2:2-13). God always has someone watching you who has the ability to bring you into your next season of blessing. Whenever possible, sow blessing into the lives of others.

The Face of Favor

The Lord bless you and keep you; the Lord make his face shine on you and be gracious to you; the Lord turn his face toward you and give you peace" (Num. 6:24-26)

1. Your Gift

a. 1 Samuel 16:14-23 - And Saul sent to Jesse, saying, Let David, I pray thee, stand before me; for he hath found favour in my sight. And it came to pass, when the evil spirit from God was upon Saul, that David took a harp, and played with his hand: so Saul was refreshed, and was well, and the evil spirit departed from him.

2. Children presented to the Lord

a. 1 Samuel 2:26 - And the child Samuel grew on, and was in favour both with the LORD, and also with men.
b. Luke 2:52 - And Jesus increased in wisdom and stature, and in favour with God and man.
c. Isaiah 54:13 - And all thy children shall be taught of the Lord; and great shall be the peace of thy children.

3. Do Good

a. Proverbs 11:27 - If you search for good, you will find favor; but if you search for evil, it will find you
b. Proverbs 12:2 - A good man obtains favor from the Lord, but a man of wicked intentions He will condemn

4. God's Word

164

a. Proverbs 3:1-4 - My son, forget not my law; but let thine heart keep my commandments: For length of days, and long life, and peace, shall they add to thee. Let not mercy and truth forsake thee: bind them about thy neck; write them upon the table of thine heart: So shalt thou find favour and good understanding in the sight of God and man.

5. Humility

a. Proverbs 3:34 - He mocks mockers, but he shows favor to the humble

6. Marriage

a. Proverbs 18:22 - Whoso findeth a wife findeth a good thing, and obtaineth favour of the LORD

7. Righteousness

a, Psalm 5:12 - For thou, LORD, wilt bless the righteous; with favour wilt thou compass him as with a shield.
b. Psalm 30:5 - For his anger endureth but a moment; in his favour is life: weeping may endure for a night, but joy cometh in the morning.

Favor in His Eyes

"But Noah found grace in the eyes of the LORD." (Genesis 6:8)

As it was in the days of Noah, so will it be at the coming of the Son of Man.

Matthew 24:37
So the angel told her, "Do not be afraid, Mary, for you have found favor with God. Luke 1:30

Just as it was in the days of Noah, so also will it be in the days of the Son of Man:

Luke 17:26
who disobeyed long ago when God waited patiently in the days of Noah, while the ark was being built. In the ark a few people, only eight souls, were saved through water.

1 Peter 3:20
And the LORD said to Moses, "I will do this very thing you have asked, for you have found favor in My sight, and I know you by name."

Exodus 33:17
As we look a little more closely at NOAH'S life, I want to point out THREE things he did that GOD found favorable.
First of all.............

I. Noah Did What Was Right When Everyone Else Was Doing Wrong

6:9 a This is the account of Noah. Noah was a righteous man, blameless among the people of his time.

1. We have already learned that NOAH lived in a society where no one did what was right in the eyes of GOD.......everyone's mind was bent on doing wrong all the time.

While everyone around him was chose to do what was RIGHT in their own eyes, NOAH choose to do what was RIGHT in GOD'S eyes.

In his book, The Cheating Culture, Don Callahan says, we are living in a time when everybody seems to think its OK to do wrong, just because everybody else is doing it.

School Students cheat on tests, because "everybody's doing it."

Athletes take steroids, because "everybody else is doing it."

People cheat on insurance claims and tax returns, because "everybody else is doing it."

"Doctors write unnecessary prescriptions, because "everybody else is doing it."

"People illegally download music and movies, because "everybody else is doing it."

Even many who claim to be Christians reject God's standard of righteousness in favor of what "feels right" for them personally or what society accepts as right.

In the EYES of GOD........RIGHT is always RIGHT and WRONG is always WRONG...........No matter how many
people are doing it.

It doesn't matter if all fifty states pass laws to legalize every type of perverse behavior known to man, from SAME-

SEX MARRIAGES to ABORTION to CHILD PORNOGRAPHY, it will never make it right.

5. If you and I are to FIND FAVOR IN THE EYES OF THE LORD we must do as NOAH did in his day and that is DO RIGHT EVEN WHEN THE WHOLE WORLD IS DOING WRONG!
Secondly.............

II. Noah Walked With God Even When No One Else Did
6:9 Noah was a righteous man, blameless along the people of his time, and he walked with God.

1. What does it mean to "walk with God?" It literally means "to walk in God's footsteps."
analogy: Did you ever walk in your dad's footsteps in the snow?
A lot of times , when a boy gets into the same career of his father, he is said to "be following in the footsteps of his dad."

When we FOLLOW someone's FOOTSTEPS it means we "stay in step" with them........."we follow their path."
SPIRITUALLY SPEAKING.........When we WALK with GOD
we "follow GOD'S footsteps" ...."we stay in step with God" ...."we follow in His path."
In NOAH'S day NO ONE was walking with GOD........everyone made his own path .
-Only NOAH walked with GOD!
-Only NOAH stayed in step with GOD! -Only NOAH followed God's footsteps!

BOY its tough to WALK WITH GOD when no one else around you does.

Some of you have the fortune of having several Christians working with you, and I'm sure you gain strength and encouragement by working
with people who share the same faith as you.

But on the other hand........some of you may work at a job
where you are the only Christian. Perhaps you are the only one who goes to church on Sundays. Perhaps you are the only one who doesn't take God's Name in vain or tell dirty jokes. Perhaps you are the only one who isn't cheating on your mate.

Let me encourage you to WALK WITH GOD even if nobody else around you does.
Illustration-----When I preaching in Illinois, we had a young teenage girl in the church named Laramie Pontious. She came from a horrible family background. Her father had physically and sexually abused her. And both her parents were alcoholics.
And yet Sunday after Sunday, Laramie would get her little brother, Monty up and get him dressed for church, and together the two of them would sit on the third pew.
My heart went out to Laramie, because she was trying to WALK WITH GOD.......even when no one else in her family did.

No matter how discouraging it may get at times KEEP WALKING WITH GOD, EVEN IF NO ONE ELSE AROUND YOU DOES! Noah did......and he found favor in the eyes of the Lord.

Noah Found Favor in the Eyes of the Lord by Doing What Was Right When Everyone Was Doing Wrong.
He Found Favor in the Eyes of the Lord by Walking With God Even When No One Else Did.

And thirdly............

III. Noah Trusted God, Even When He Didn't Understand

1. In verses 11-21, GOD reveals to NOAH His plan to destroy the world.

In verse 17, GOD told NOAH he was going to do this by bringing a FLOOD upon the earth. NOAH had never seen or heard of a flood before........As a matter of fact, no one on earth had ever even seen RAIN before.

In verses 14-16, GOD gave NOAH specific instructions for building this huge boat, which was as long as three football fields and as high as a three story building. NOAH had never heard of an ARK before.

In verse 22, GOD told NOAH he wanted him to take TWO of EVERY KIND of ANIMAL on board this big boat, along with the seven members of his family. NOAH didn't understand just how he was supposed to GET these ANIMALS on the ARK.

As a matter-of-fact, NOAH didn't understand ANY of GOD'S plan.........but notice VERSE 22 Noah did everything just as God commanded him.

2. In your life and mine, there are times when everything in side of us is crying out........."God, this doesn't make a bit of sense!"

-GOD is telling us NO......when everything inside us is saying YES.

-GOD is telling us to WAIT.......when everything inside us is telling us to GO AHEAD.

-GOD is telling us to LEAVE IT ALONE.......when everything inside us is telling us to TAKE IT.

-GOD is telling us NOW IS NOT THE TIME.....when everything inside us is telling us NOW IS THE BEST TIME.

3. There will always be TIMES when we DO not understand GOD'S plan.......or....His timing........or His Ways.........BUT GOD doesn't ask to UNDERSTAND, HE asks us to TRUST HIM and OBEY HIM.

4. DAY after DAY for 120 Years, NOAH worked on that ARK ....perhaps without ever fully understanding what was to come, and yet HE trusted GOD and obeyed him, by doing everything GOD commanded him to do.
And Noah Found Favor in the Eyes of the Lord.

Thanksgiving Prayer For Favor

1. I thank You Lord for sparing my life to this moment. I know that there is hope for me. I refuse to give up in Jesus name.
2. I thank You father for all blessings You have given me in the time past.
3. Lord God Almighty, I thank You for the favor I enjoy as a child of God.
4. Father, I confess every sin; personal or ancestral that has invited. disfavour and rejection into my life at some point. I ask for forgiveness through the blood of Jesus.
5. Let the powerful blood of Jesus visit my foundation and do a thorough cleansing in the name of Jesus.
6. Every seed of rejection, hatred and failure in my life, I command you to be consumed by the fire of God in the name of Jesus.
7. Lord, perfume my life with the aroma of favor in the name of Jesus.
8. Father let your strength be made perfect in my weakness. Let your grace be sufficient for me in the name of Jesus.
9. I receive divine favor to excel at every examination, interview and tests in the name of Jesus.
10. Lord you caused Esther to be preferred above others, cause me to be preferred above my competitors in the name of Jesus.
11. Let our Children and youths find favor in your sight after the order of Daniel in the name of Jesus.
12. Let me obtain favor in the sight of everyone you have ordained to help me fulfil my destiny in the name of Jesus.

13. Let the wings of favor catapult me to the right place at the right time in the name of Jesus.
14. Lord, give my Ahasuerus a sleepless night until he has given me my due reward in Jesus name
15. Let your favor usher in a harvest of revival in our church, city and nation in the name of Jesus.
16. I release the Spirit of truth and mercy over this land and her people in the mighty name of Jesus
17. Lord, bring about the set time to favor this land in all its length and breadth in Jesus
18. Father, perfume my life, so I can have flavor in Jesus name.
19. Father, let your flavor in my life lead me to great favors in the name of Jesus.
20. Lord, single me out with your anointing of favor in the name of Jesus.
21. Today, I enter into every opportunity created by God's favor for me in Jesus name.
22. Every power contending with my divine destiny, scatter unto desolation, in the name of Jesus.
23. I declare my graduation from the school of struggle and suffering in the mighty name of Jesus
24. Every mark of disfavor upon my destiny be erased by the blood of Jesus.
25. I will not labour in vain nor bring forth for trouble. Whatever I lay my hands upon shall prosper in the name of Jesus.
26. By unusual favor of God, my church shall begin to enjoy exponential growth in the name of Jesus.
27. Father, Let the door of utterance, faith and ministration be opened unto Victory House in different parts of the world in the mighty name of Jesus.

28. Father I thank you for anointing my life so I can begin to shine and bring light of favor to the world in the name of Jesus. t
29. In this year 2020 O Lord, let stand on top of my mountain in the name of Jesus
30. I receive the grace to overcome impossibilities and to live in the realm of possibilities in the name of Jesus.
31. Lord, surround me with favor like a shield in the name of Jesus.
32. Lord, surround me with unstoppable favor this year in the name of Jesus
33. You O Lord are my King, as Esther obtained favor before the king, I obtain favor before you in Jesus' mighty name

Prophetic & Apostolic Coving

The Prophetic Prayer's & Apostolic coving for the 2020 year of "UNSTOPABLE FAVOR"

Moses said to the people, "Do not fear, for God has come to test you, that the fear of him may be before you, that you may not sin." Exodus 20:20

Only the trees that you know are not trees for food you may destroy and cut down, that you may build siegeworks against the city that makes war with you, until it falls. Deuteronomy 20:20

And the men of Israel went out to fight against Benjamin, and the men of Israel drew up the battle line against them at Gibeah. Judges 20:20

And I will shoot three arrows to the side of it, as though I shot at a mark.

1 Samuel 20:20
Joab answered, "Far be it from me, far be it, that I should swallow up or destroy!

2 Samuel 20:20
And each struck down his man. The Syrians fled, and Israel pursued them, but Ben-hadad king of Syria escaped on a horse with horsemen. 1 Kings 20:20

The rest of the deeds of Hezekiah and all his might and how he made the pool and the conduit and brought water into the city, are they not written in the Book of the Chronicles of the Kings of Judah? 2 Kings 20:20

I have been crucified with Christ. It is no longer I who live, but Christ who lives in me. And the life I now live in the flesh I live by faith in the Son of God, who loved me and gave himself for me. Galatians 2:20

For by works of the law no human being will be justified in his sight, since through the law comes knowledge of sin. Romans 3:20

I welcome you into your own year of Holy Spirit: My Help on every side in Jesus Mighty name.

1. Father, my exceeding greatness will not be undermined throughout this year and beyond, in Jesus Name. (Isaiah 54:3, Zechariah 1:18-21)
2. Father, let my head be lifted above all my enemies on every side, in Jesus Name. (Psalm 30:1)
3. Father, let my mouth be enlarged over all my mockers by making my life exceedingly great, in Jesus Name. (1 Samuel 2:1)
4. Father, let every step that I take, in this year, cause me to move forward, in Jesus Name. (Proverbs 4:18, 2 Corinthians 3:18)
5. Father, let every small project and effort that I undertake, in this year, lead me into abundant greatness, in Jesus Name. (Job 8:7)
6. Father, let all my long-term desires for change and greatness be granted in this year, in Jesus Name. (Job 6:8)
7. Father, let all the blessings that you gave me, in previous years, be added unto me. None of my past achievements

shall fall apart, in this year, in Jesus Name. (Psalm 115:13-14)

8. Father, take away every stumbling block to my Agenda of Exceeding Greatness throughout 2020 and beyond, in Jesus Name. (Isaiah 57:14, Job 12:14, Revelations 3:7)

9. Father, let our Agenda of this year for our our church "Families" be personally and visibly confirmed in my own life and in all the things that I do in this year, in Jesus Name. (2 Kings 7:1-3, Mark 16:20)

10. Father, let me and my family members be spared and protected from all evil works, destructions and reproaches, in this year, in Jesus Name. (Psalm 91:1-16, Joel 2:17)

11. Father, let all the mouths of my enemies and the mockers of my faith, in Christ Jesus, be permanently shut by the reasons of your undeniable favor in 2020, in Jesus Name. (Psalm 86:13-17)

12. Father, let every device of the wicked, targeted against my life, be destroyed throughout the year, in Jesus Name. (Job 5:12-13, Isaiah 54:17

13. Father, cause my feet not to meet with wicked and unreasonable men and women and destiny destroyers throughout the year and beyond, in Jesus Name. (2 Thessalonians 3:2-3)

14. Father, as I obey your word, make me to be above all challenges and circumstances throughout the year, in Jesus Name. (Deuteronomy 28:1)

15. Father, let me enjoy unparalleled and accelerated increase in all my endeavors throughout year, in Jesus Name. (Deuteronomy 28:4)

16. Father, let your goodness and mercy accompany me throughout my journey in this year, in Jesus Name. (Psalm 23:6)

17. Father, add all the good things of life to me daily throughout the year. I shall not lack any good thing as I serve and seek you, in Jesus Name. (Psalm 34:10, Exodus 23:25-26, Mathew 6:33)

18. Father, let me enjoy your divine presence from the beginning of the year until the end, culminating in "my unlimited progress", "my unspeakable joy" and "my uninterrupted peace", in Jesus Name. (Deuteronomy 11:12)

19. Father, by the blood of Jesus, let my life and my entire household be preserved and exempted from all trouble and troublemakers in the year, in Jesus Name. (Galatians 6:17)

20. Father, let all people acknowledge the undeniable aura of your blessings upon my life, throughout the year and beyond, in Jesus Name. (Isaiah 61:9)

21. Father, let there be no single occurrence of loss of life, property or material blessings in my family. Let only the voices of joy, gladness and thanksgiving become a daily routine throughout the year, in Jesus Name. (Isaiah 51:3, Numbers 31:49)

22. Father, I cover myself and my entire family with the blood of Jesus against the arrows of the devil and his agents throughout the year, in Jesus Name. (Zechariah 9:11)

23. Father, let my mouth be filled with laughter and my tongue with singing throughout the year, in Jesus Name. (Psalm 126:2)

24. Father, let me enjoy angelic protection in all my journeys, "going out and coming in," throughout the year, in Jesus Name. (Psalm 91:11)

SALVATION PRAYER

Give your life to the Lord.

Dear Friend, if you just prayed this prayer, I would like to welcome you into the family of God! Your sins are forgiven!

Father, I come to you in the precious name of your Son, Jesus. You said in Your Word that if I confess with my mouth that Jesus Christ is my Lord and my Savior and I believe in my heart that God has raised Him from the dead, I will be saved. I make the decision today to surrender every area of my life to the lordship of Jesus.

Jesus, come into my heart. Take out the stony heart and put in a heart of flesh. I turn my back on the world and on sin. I repent and I put my trust in You. I acknowledge that I am a sinner. I would like to thank You for dying on the cross for my sin and shedding Your blood for me so that I might be forgiven of my sin. Thank You that You rose from the dead and that one day, You are coming back for me. I confess that Jesus Christ has come in the flesh and that He is my personal Lord and Savior. Thank you, Lord Jesus, for saving me. I accept by faith the free gift of salvation. Amen (so be it).

Dear Friend, if you just prayed this prayer, I would like to welcome you into the family of God! Your sins are forgiven! This is the good news of the gospel of the Lord Jesus Christ. You are now a child of God and you will live with Him forever. I encourage you to do several things to get to know Him. Read your Bible and pray everyday (talk to Jesus about everything in your life). Find a Bible-believing church that believes in the lordship of Jesus Christ. Be around strong believers who will encourage you and lift you up in your walk with God. Tell someone about your new-found faith and joy that only Jesus can bring.

Here is an effective way of sharing Jesus with others. Simply read it to your friends, family, and others and watch what the Lord will do.

Dr. Sheka Mansaray is the founder and Presiding Bishop of "Faith Embassy International Ministries (Revelation Church)" a multi- cultural, non-denominational church in Maryland USA.

Dr. Mansaray is the founder of Dr. Sheka Mansaray Ministries International, a partnership-based outreach ministry with a solid Apostolic and Prophetic Mandate.

Dr. Sheka Mansaray is also the founder of "Alpha Business Network" a network of current and future business owners. He is also The founder Presiding Bishop of Bishop's & Apostles International network a platform that raising up leaders in the body of Christ to rebuild the walls that is broken in the church.

Dr. Mansaray is a gifted Poet, Writer, Philanthropist, Entrepreneur, and Author.

Dr. Sheka Mansaray is a husband, happily married to his Beautiful wife, Nanah Mansaray; and a father to their three children, daughter, Faith Mansaray; and Son, Sheka Jeremiah Mansaray Jr. and son, Joseph Ezekiel Mansaray.

Books by the Author Dr. Sheka Mansaray

1. The Tears of My Father: (My Gift to the World)
2. Desert Rose : (WORDS FOR THOUGHTS)
3. Warfare Time: (Spiritual Warfare)
4. Carrier of Christ's Light: Arise, shine, for your light has come
5. Revelation Today (Living A life of Faith Daily Vol-1)
6. Unveiling Prosperity (INSIGHT OF PROSPERITY Vol 1)
7. Unveiling Prosperity (Curse & Blessing Vol 2)
8. Unveiling Prosperity (SPIRIT OF POVERTY Vol 3)
9. Revelation Today: (New oil daily Vol 2)
10. Pay yourself (steps to wealth)
11. Blessings of Wealth (Resource Creates Resource)
12. The Holy Spirit: (My Helper)
13 prayer Ammunition
14. Unveiled Faces: Fasting & Praying Manuel
15.Unstoppable favor: God's Plan & God's way

www.ingramcontent.com/pod-product-compliance
Lightning Source LLC
Chambersburg PA
CBHW051423090426
42737CB00014B/2809